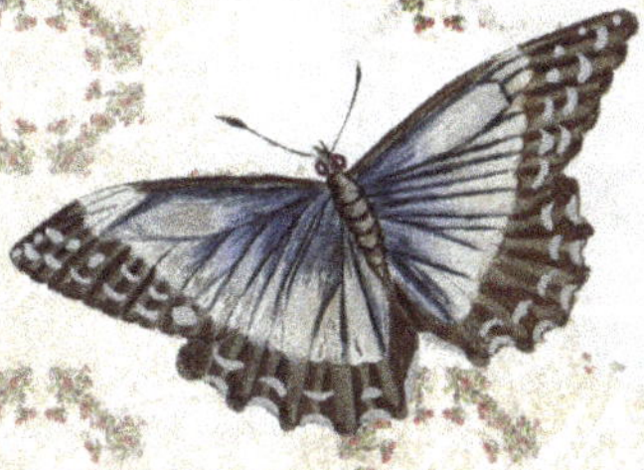

Alice in Wonderland

An illustrated journal in full color

KATIE MACALISTER

L.K. GLOVER

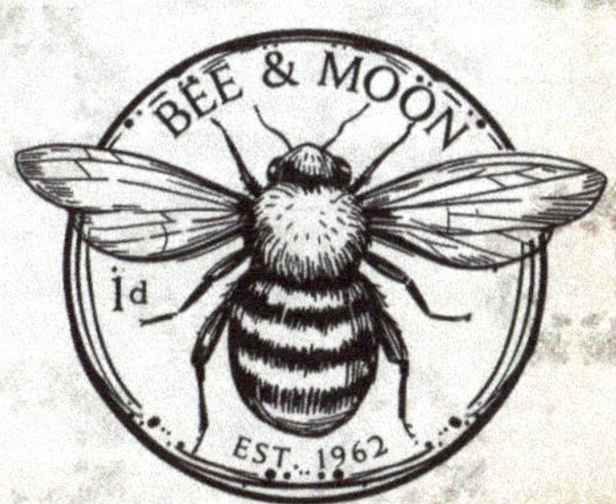

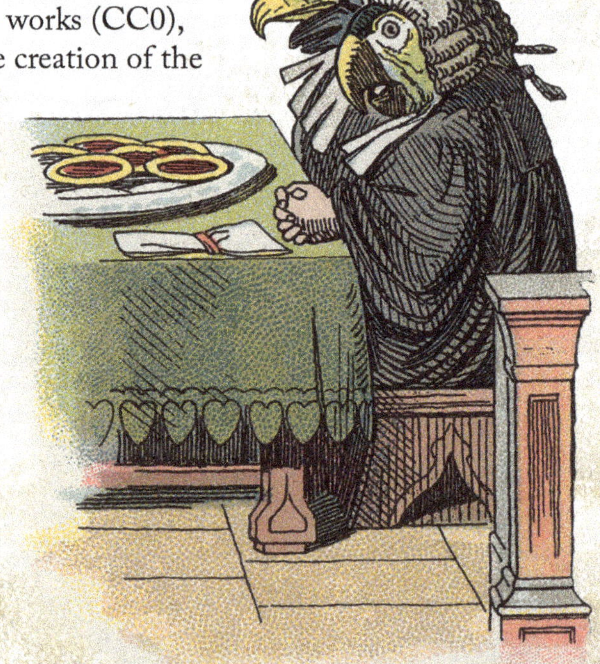

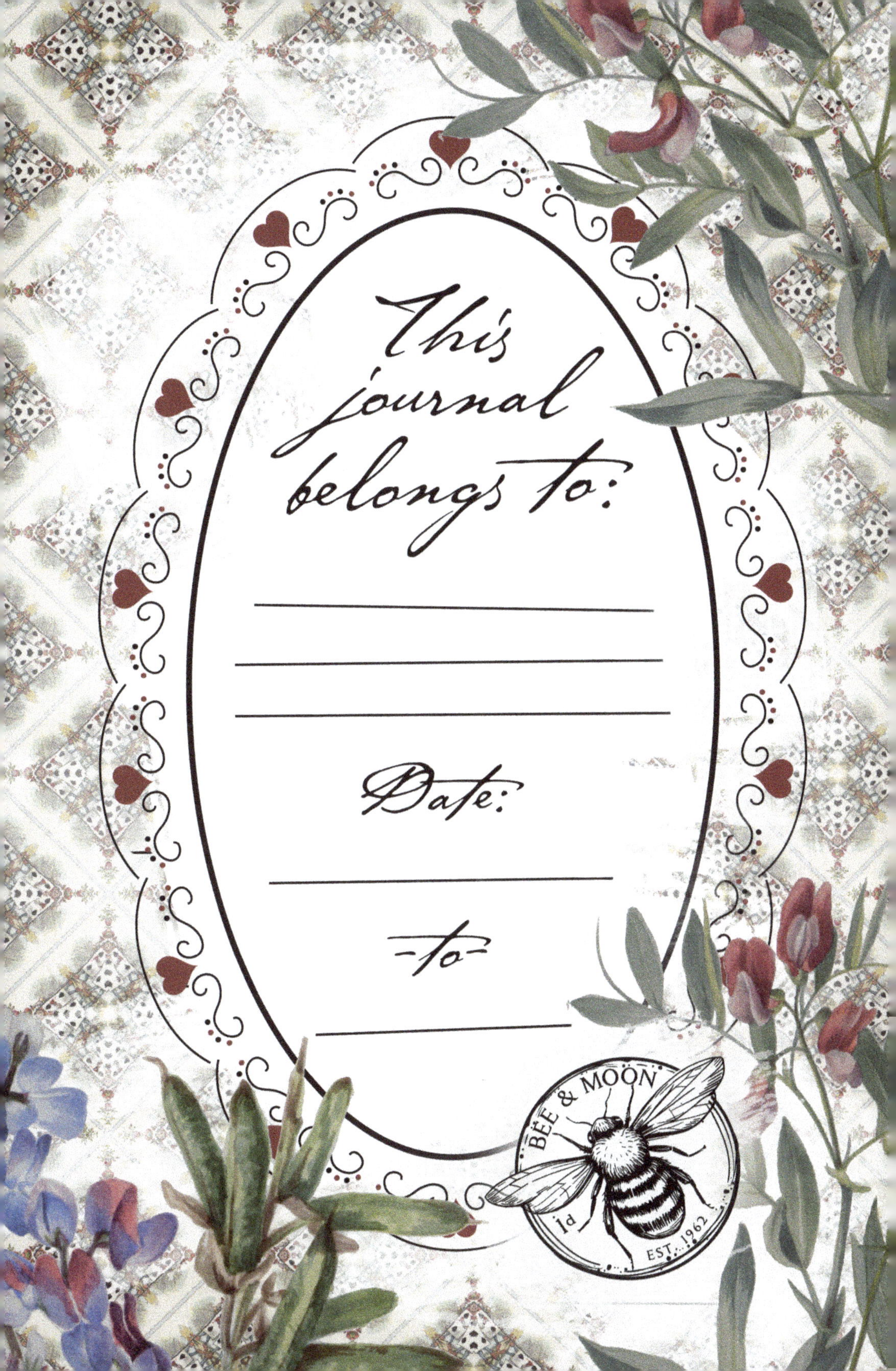

This
journal
belongs to:
Date:
-to-
BEE & MOON
EST. 1962
1d

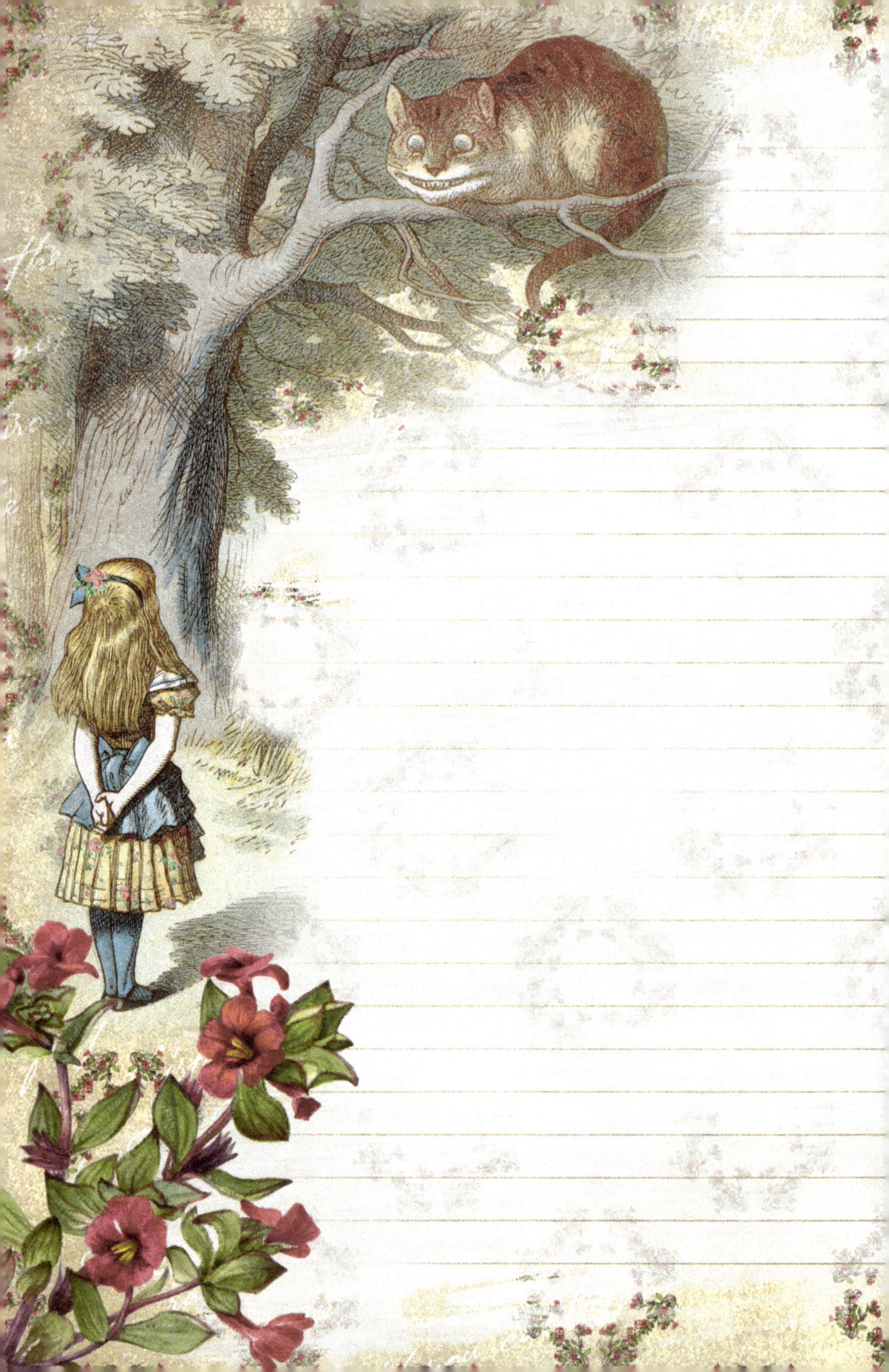

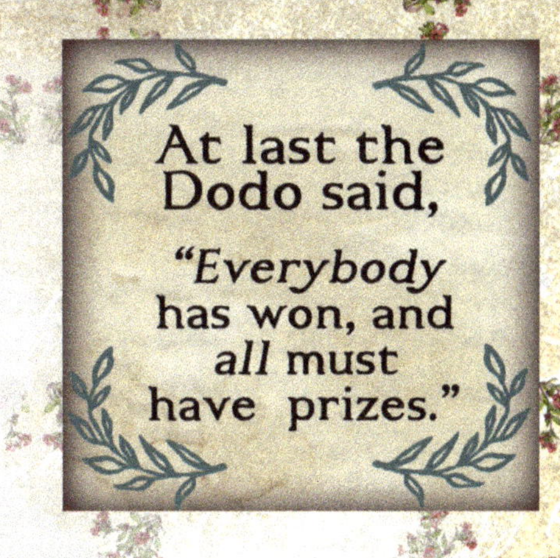
At last the
Dodo said,

"Everybody
has won, and
all must
have prizes."

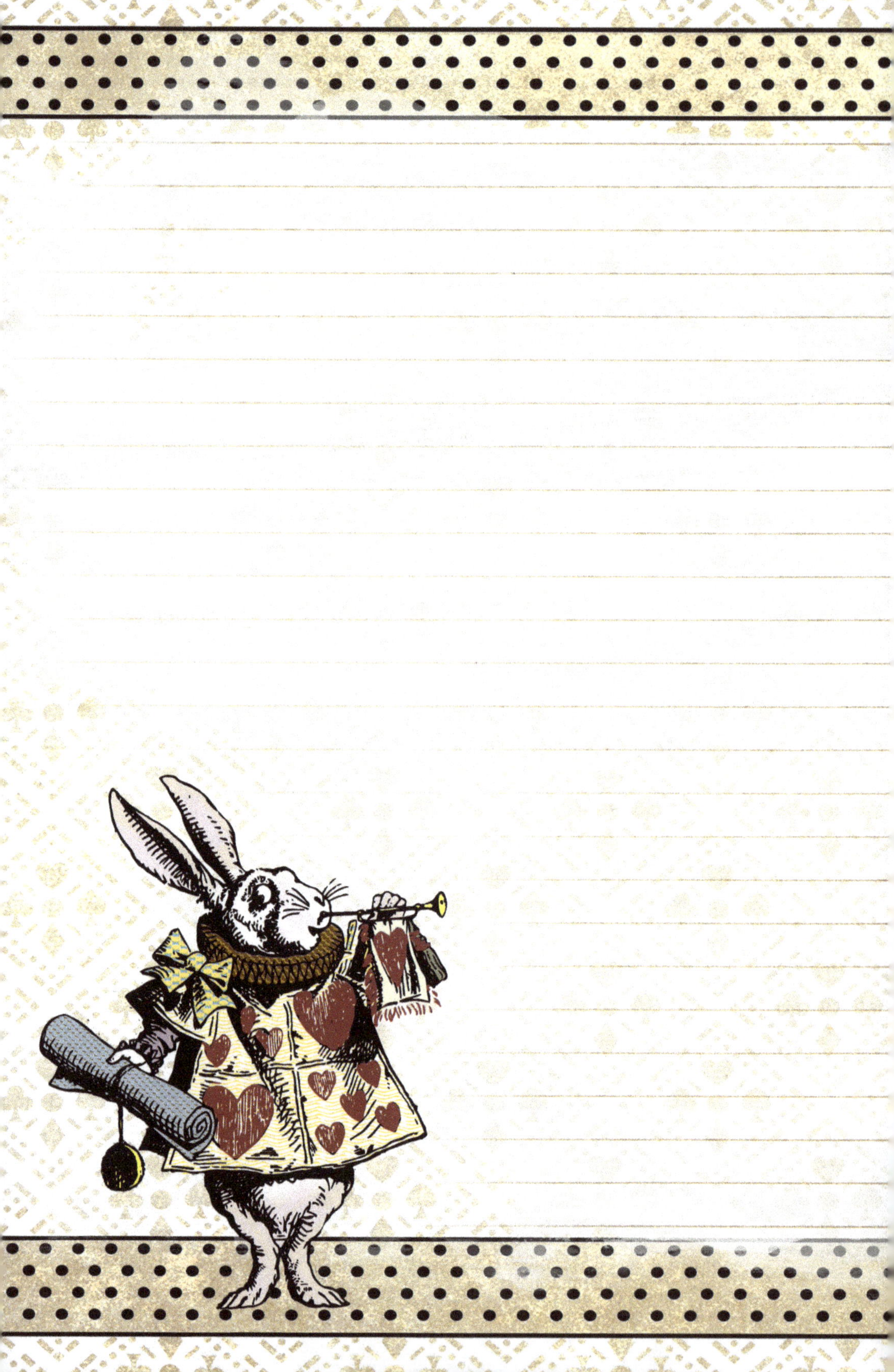

Why, sometimes I've believed as many
as six impossible things before breakfast.

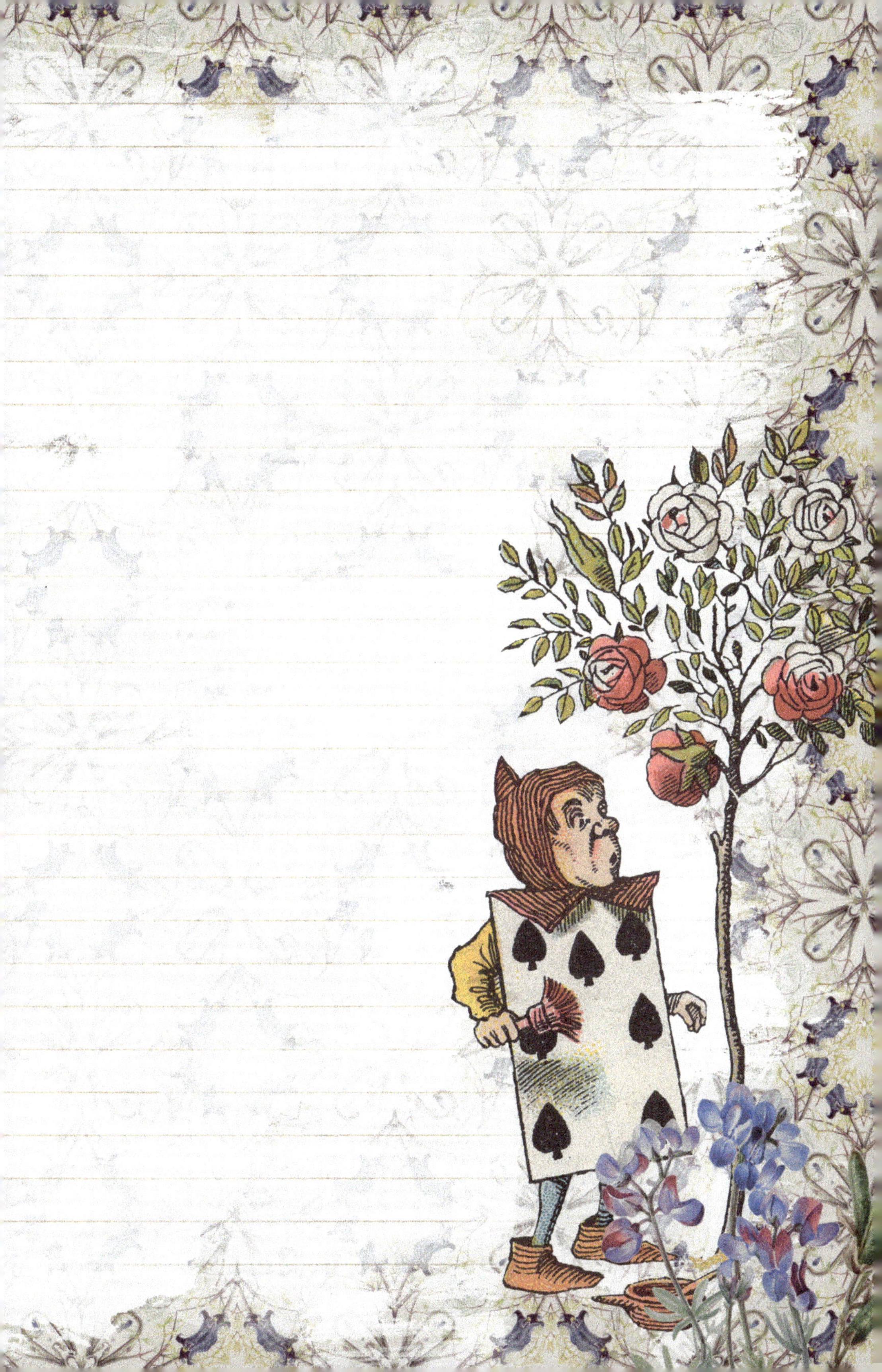

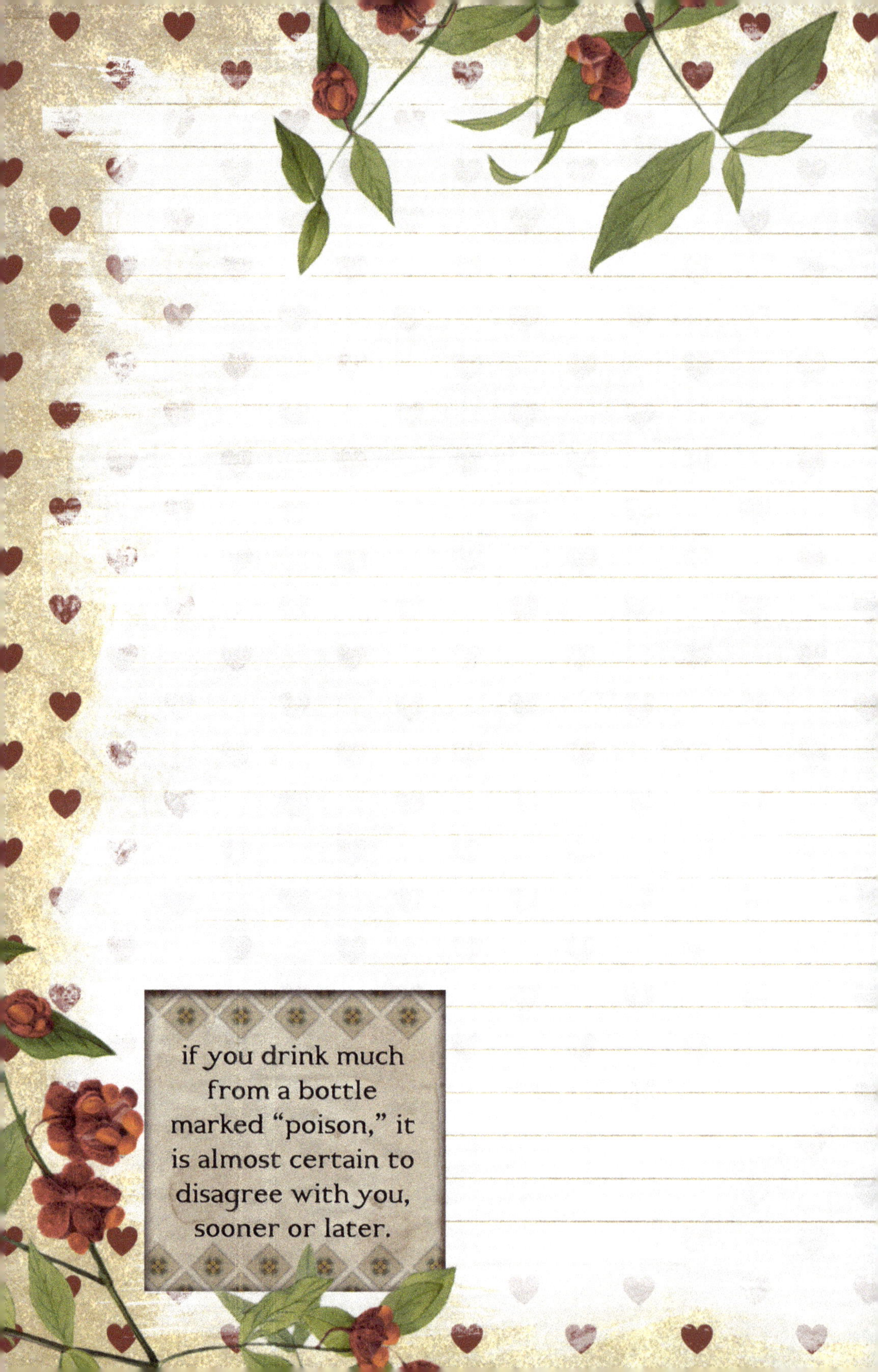

if you drink much
from a bottle
marked "poison," it
is almost certain to
disagree with you,
sooner or later.

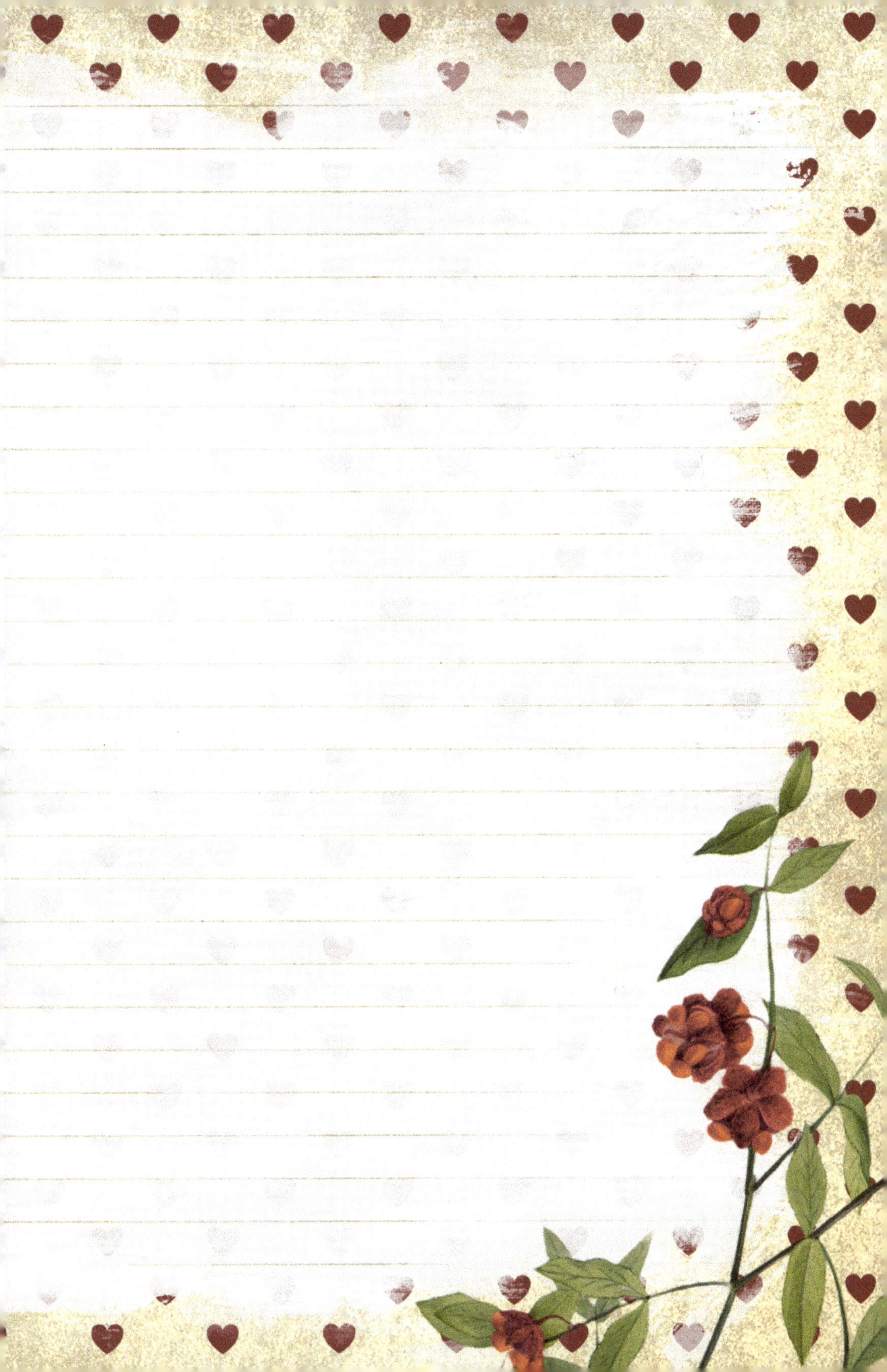

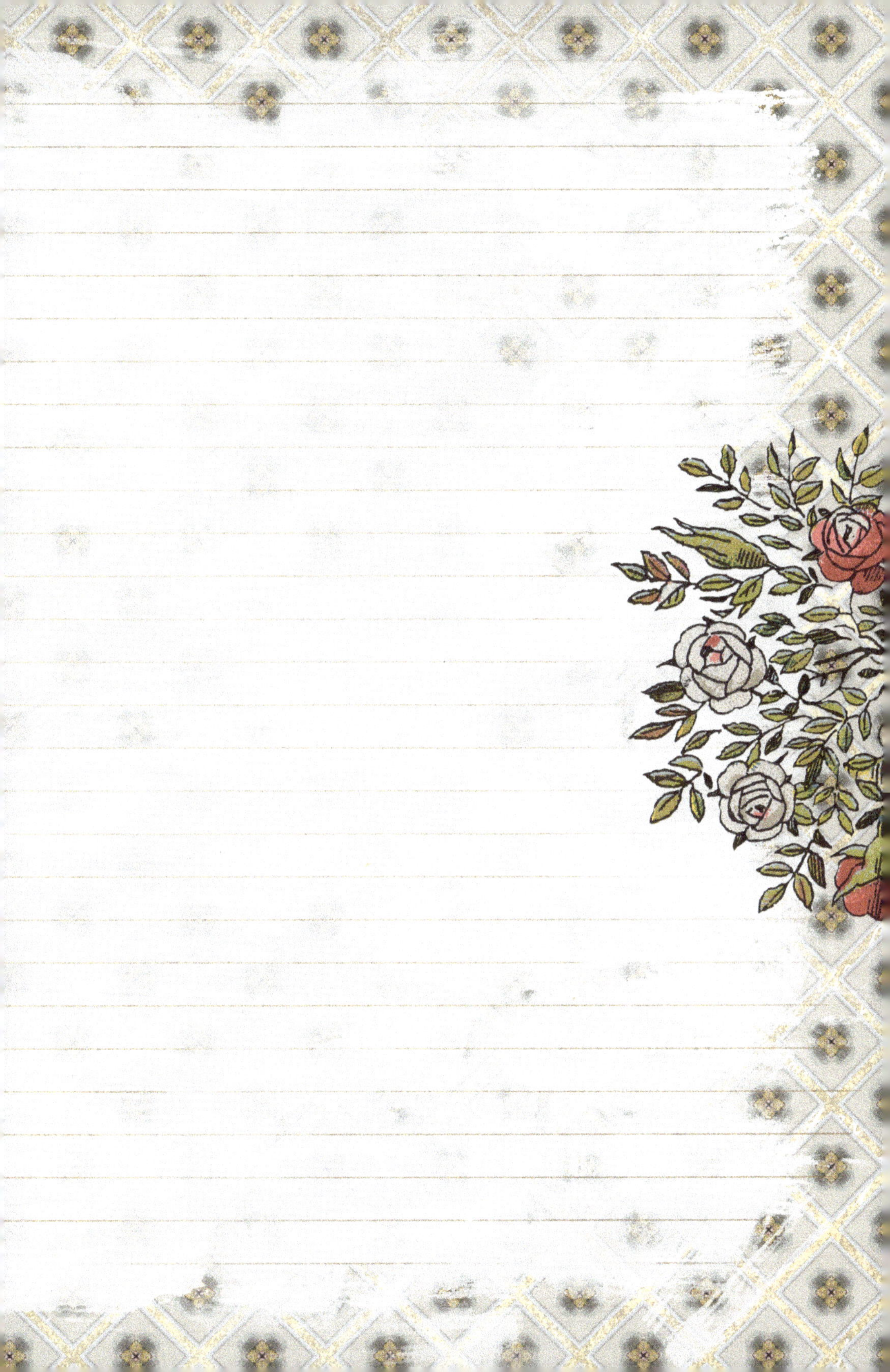

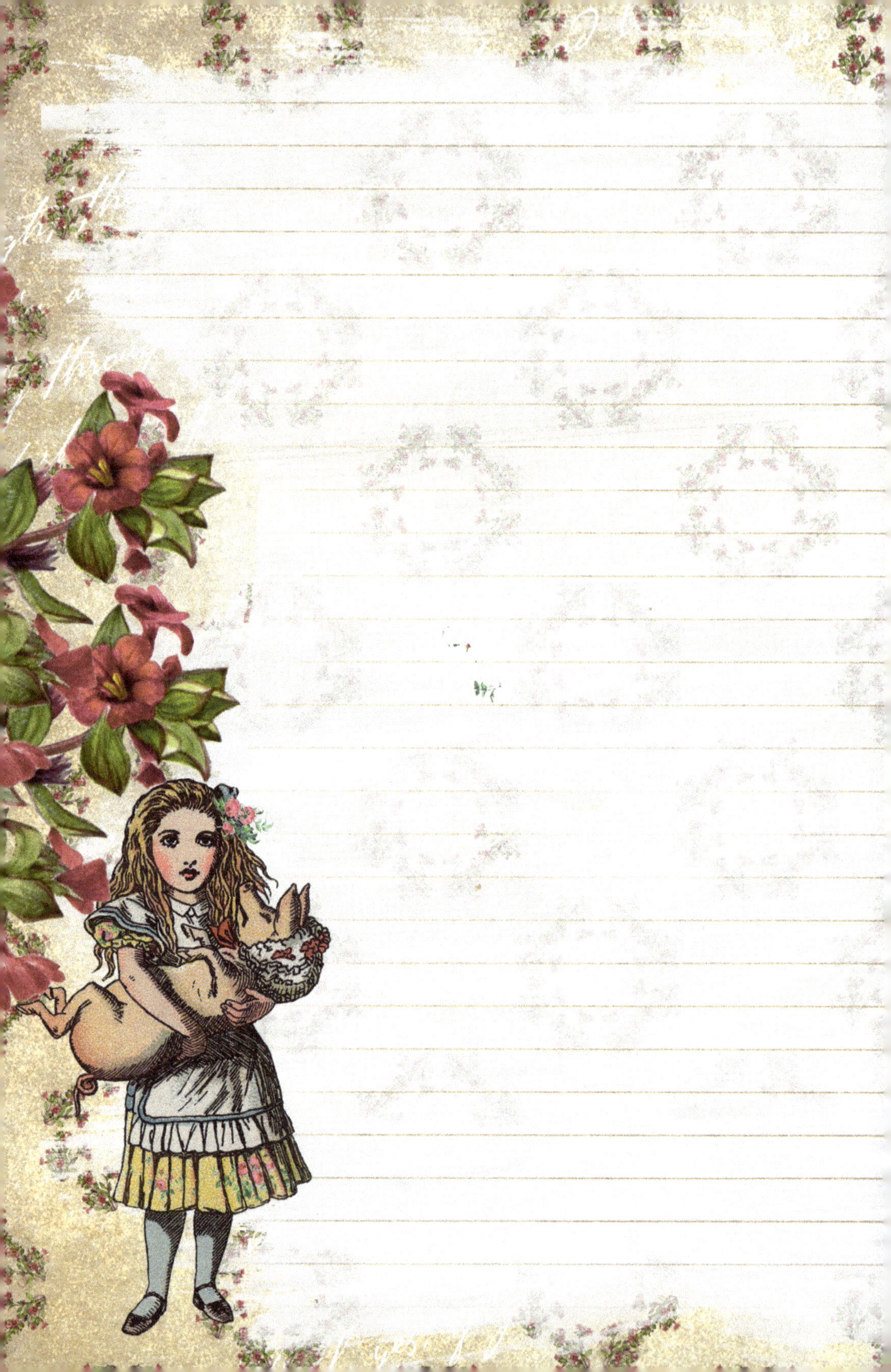

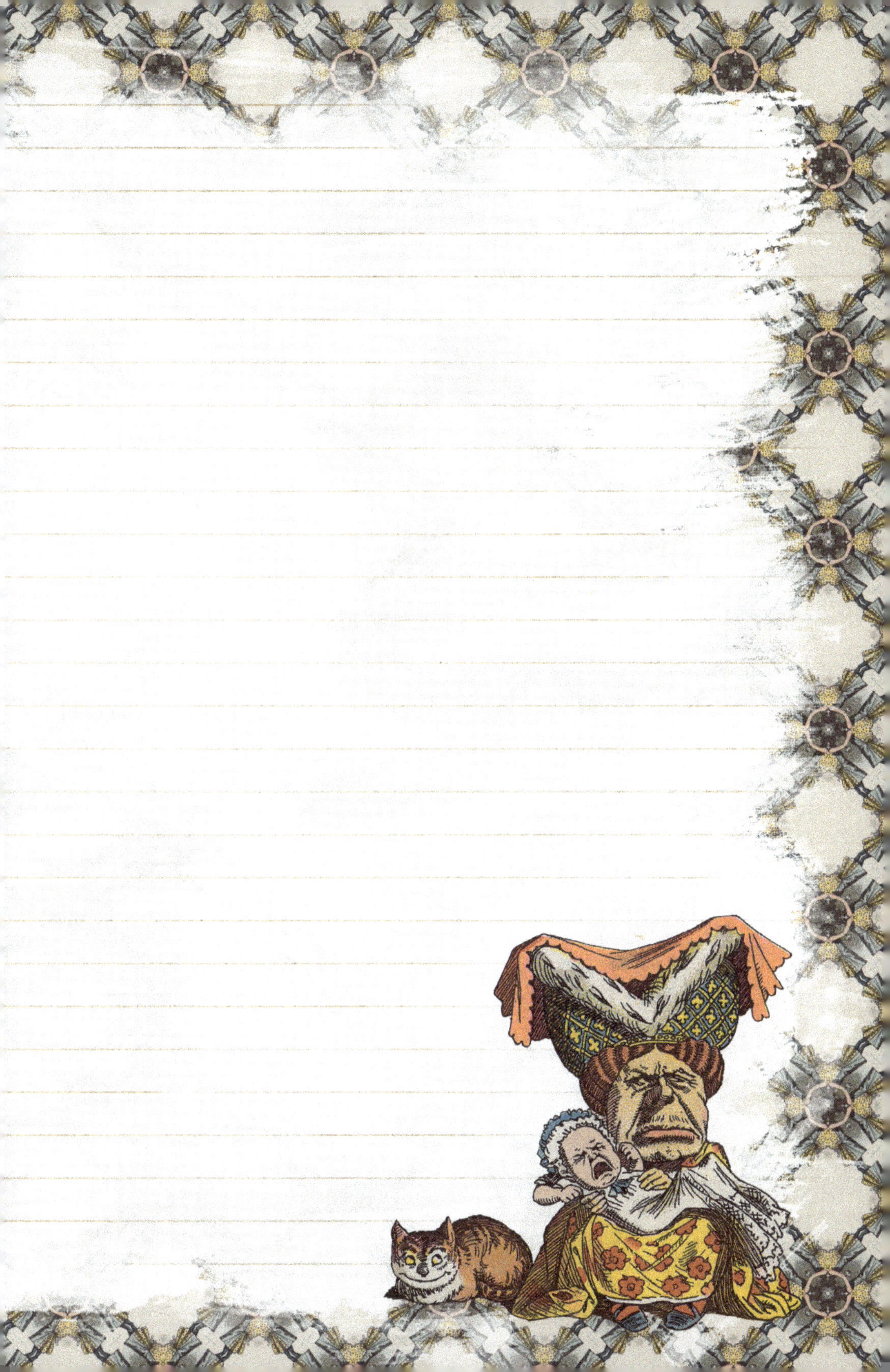

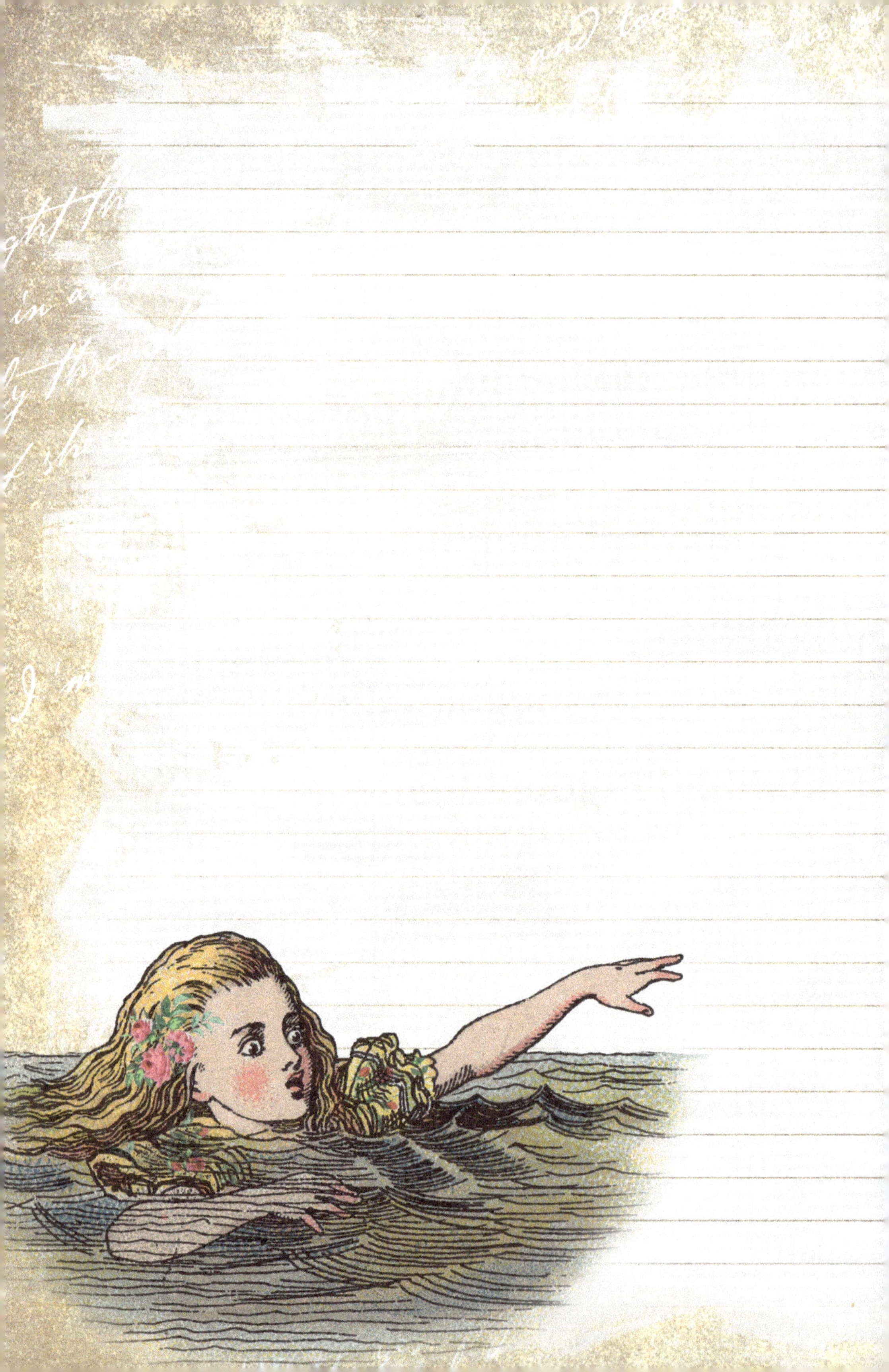

Oh, 'tis love, 'tis love, that makes the world go round!

"It must be a very pretty dance," said Alice timidly.

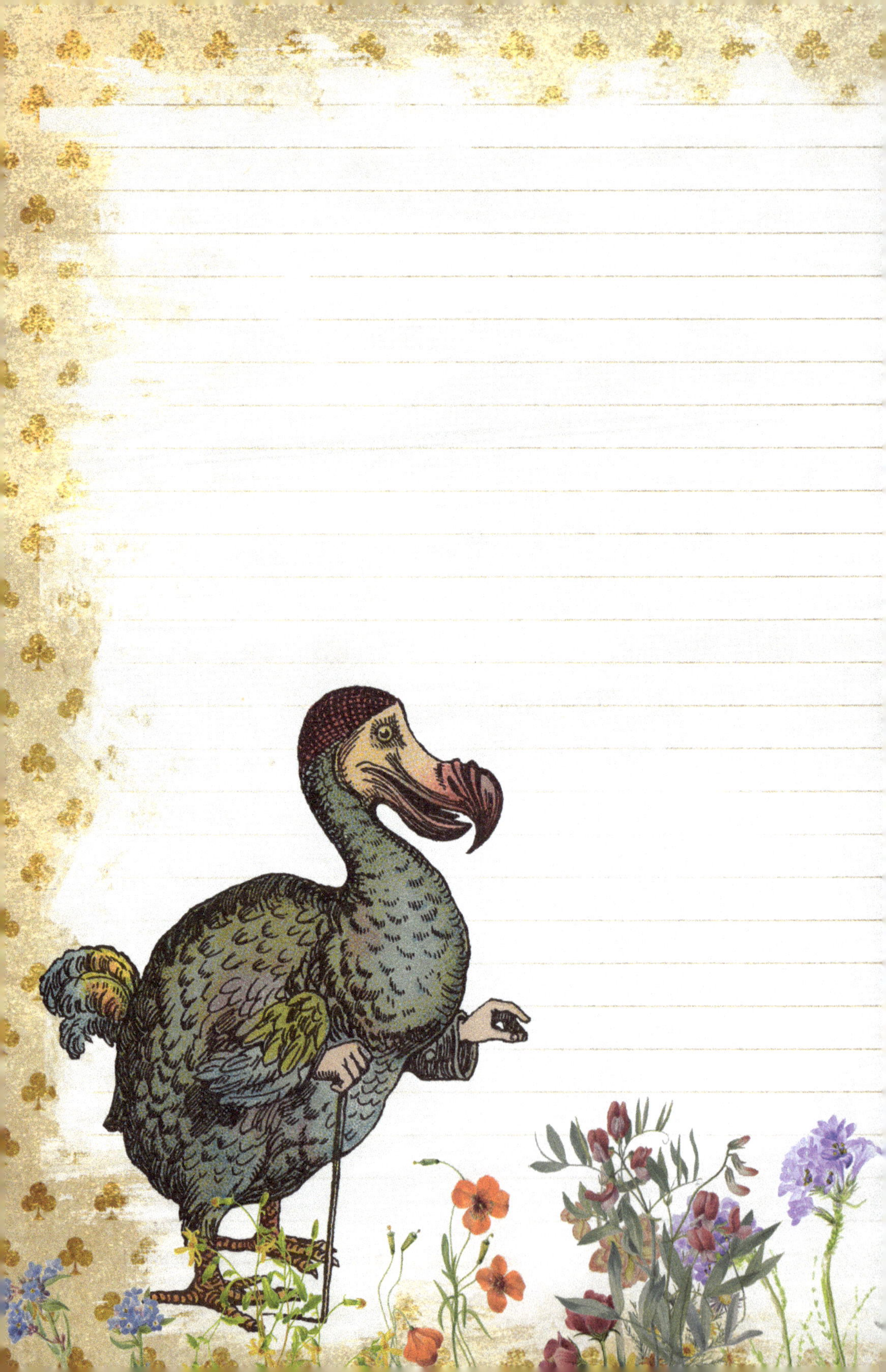

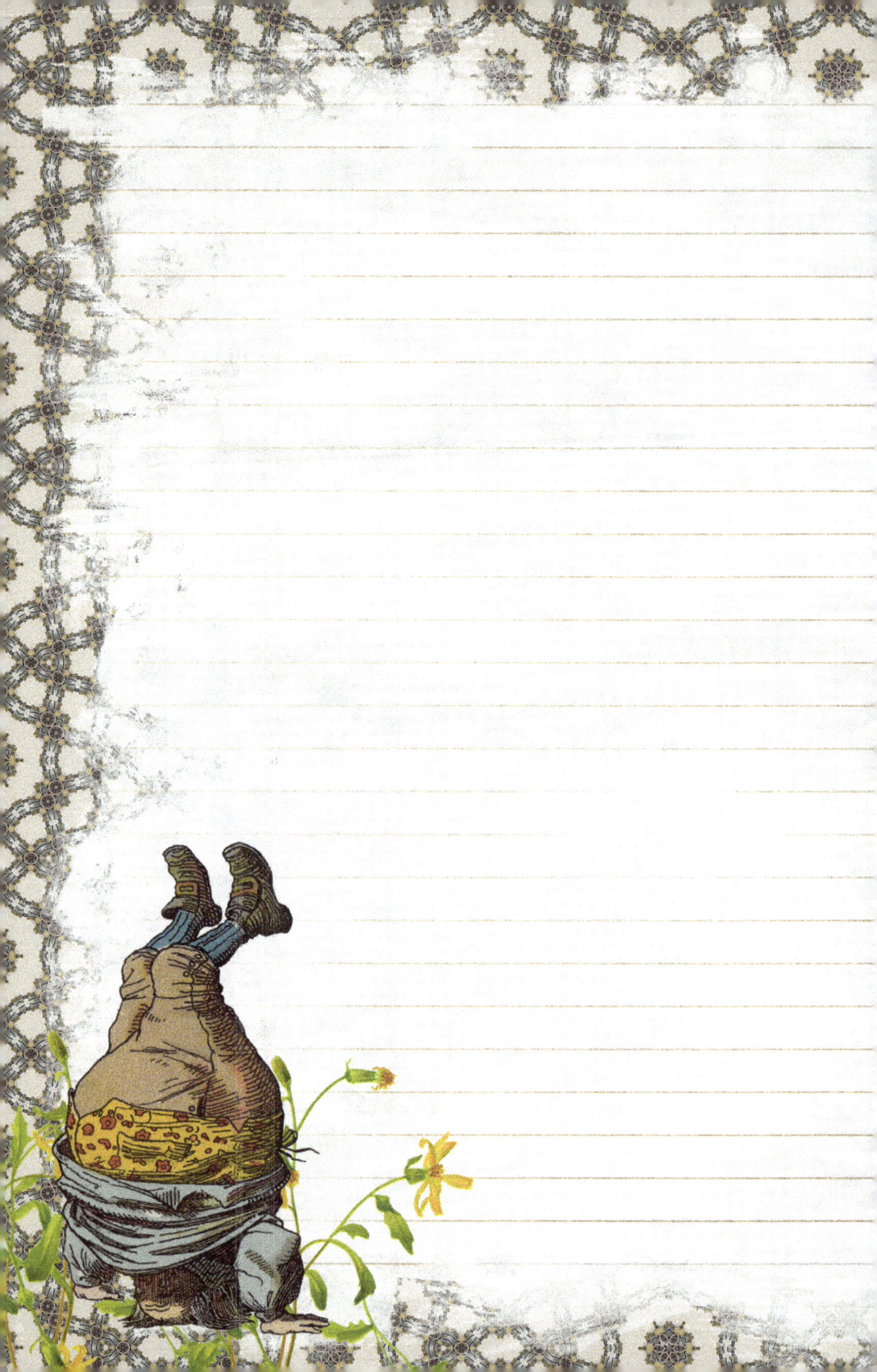

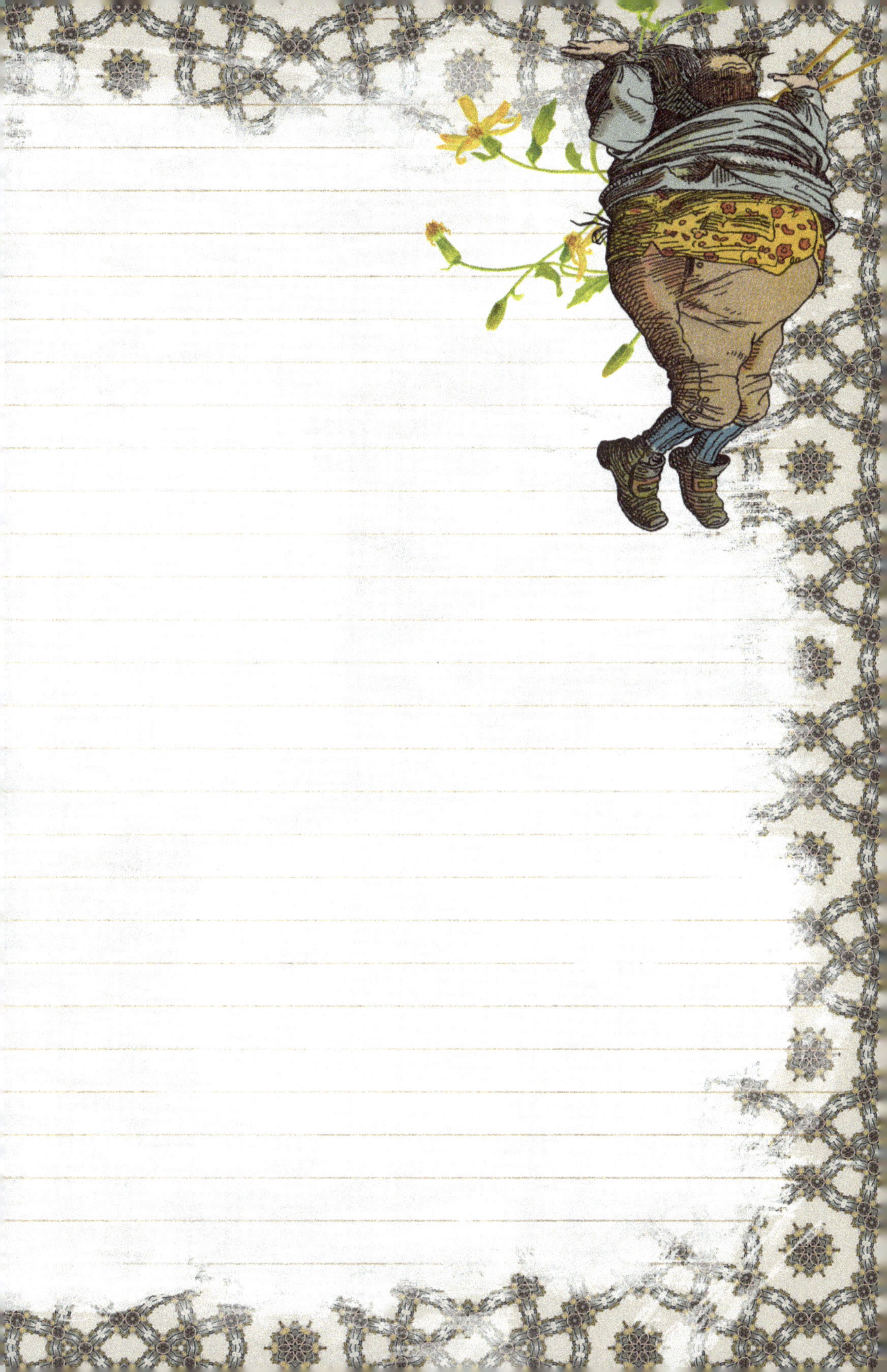

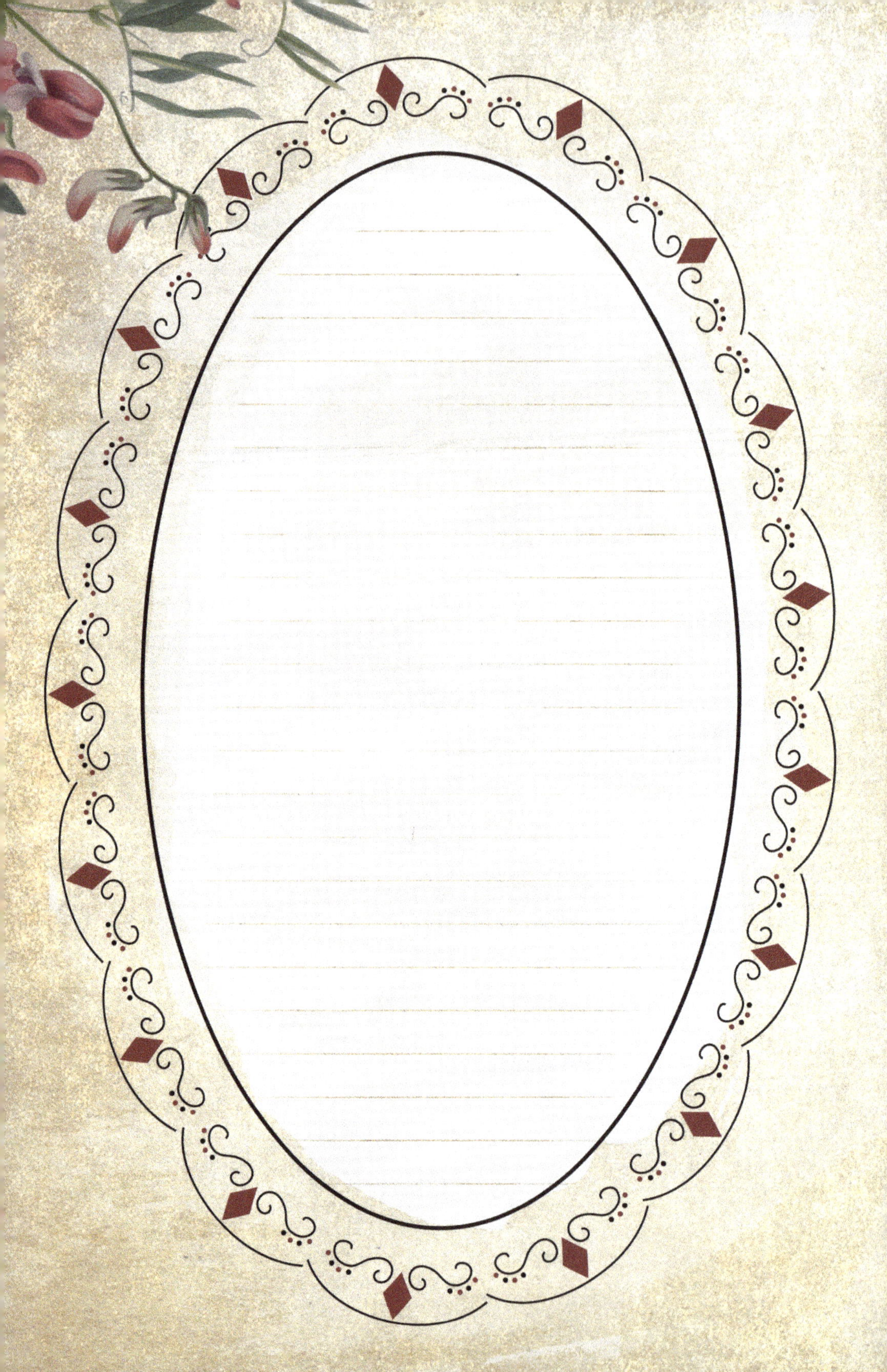

DRINK ME

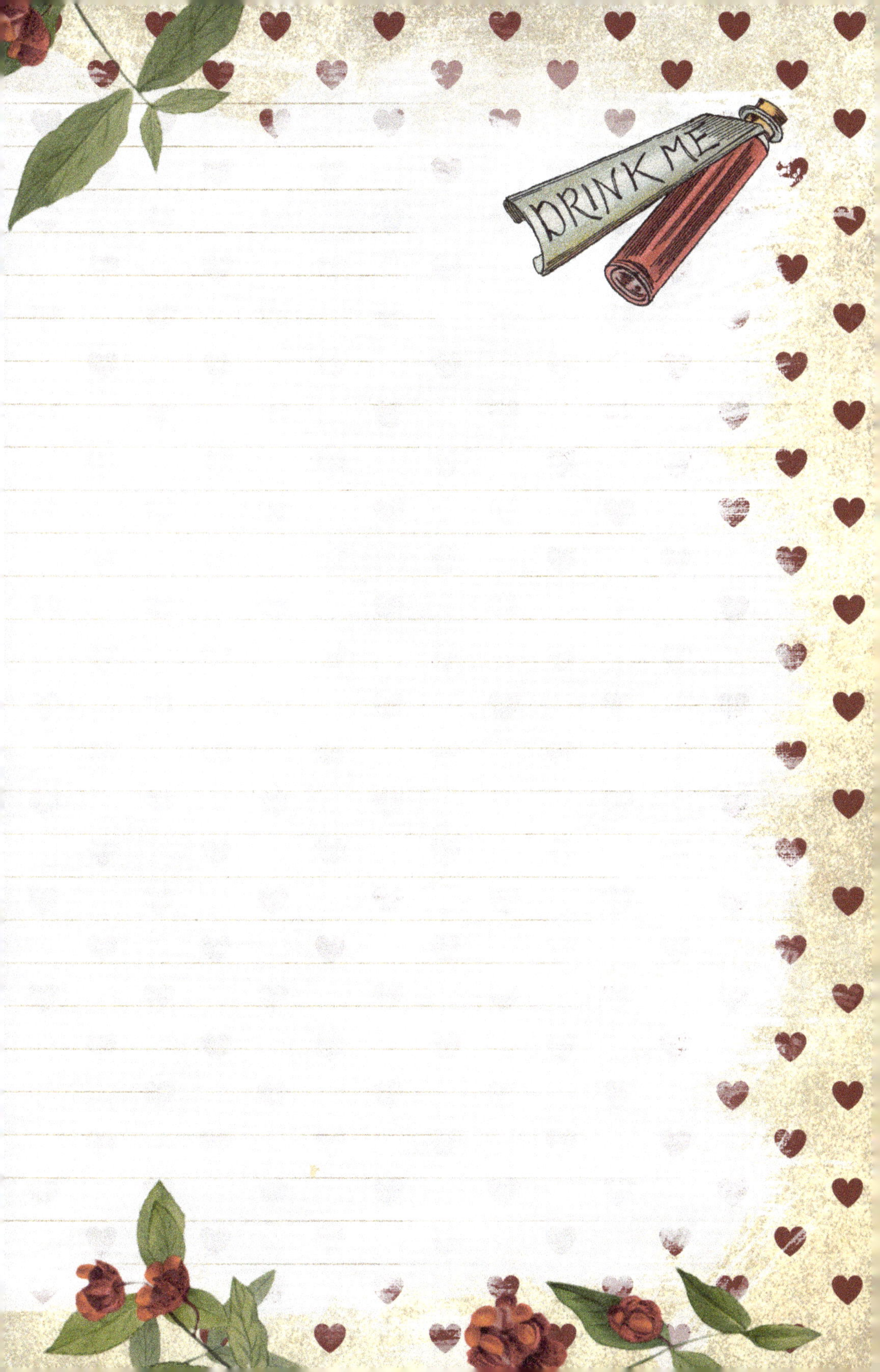
DRINK ME

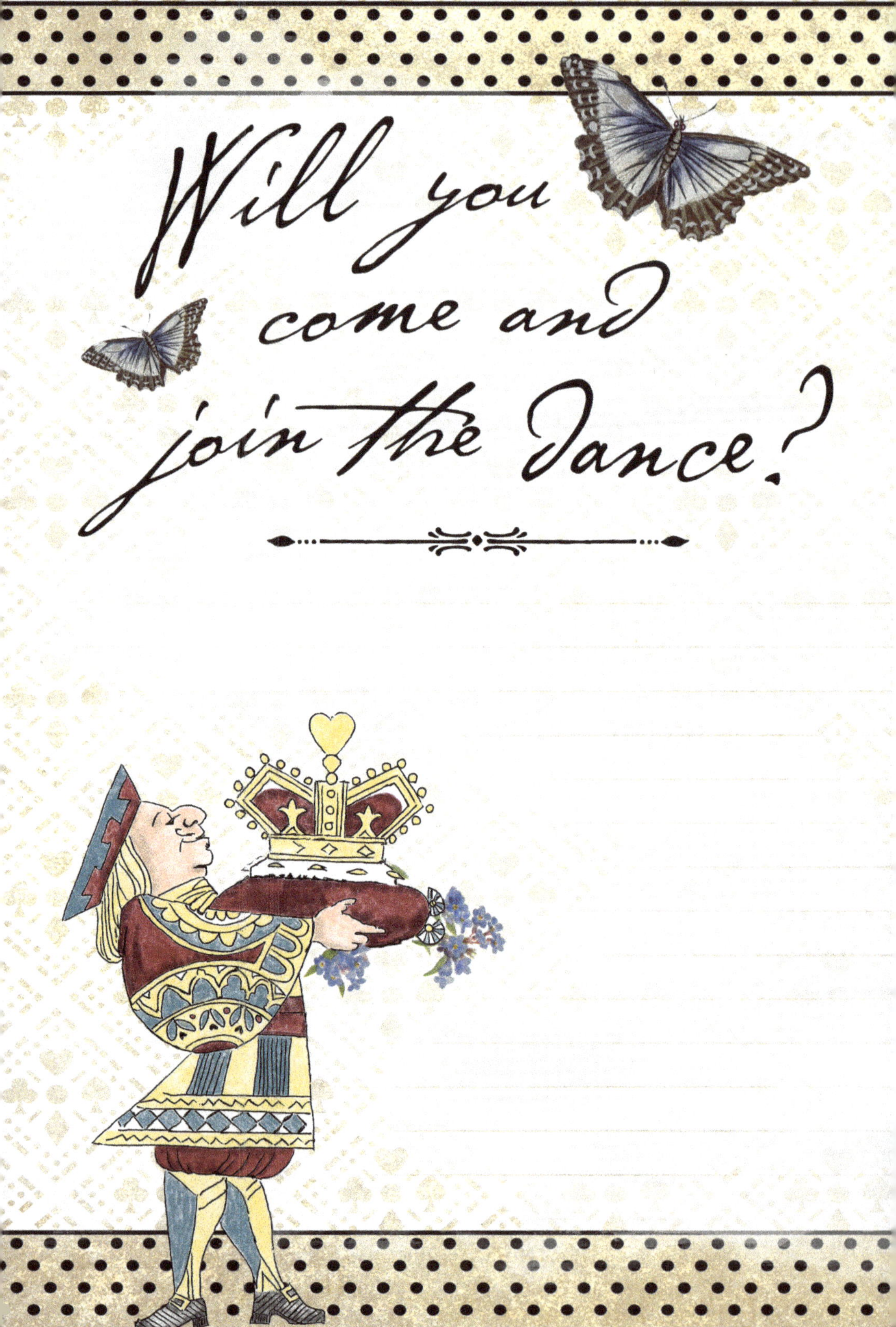

Will you
come and
join the dance?

Will you, won't you,
will you, won't you,
will you
join the dance?

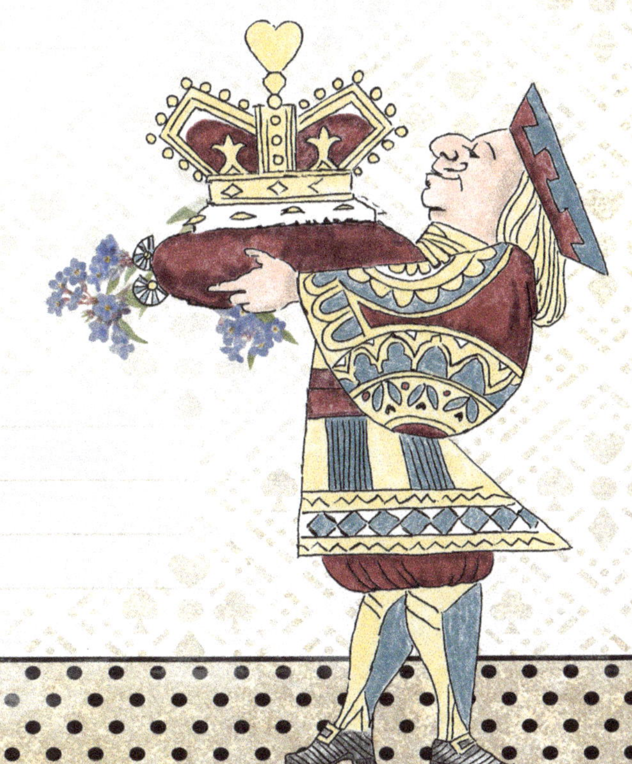

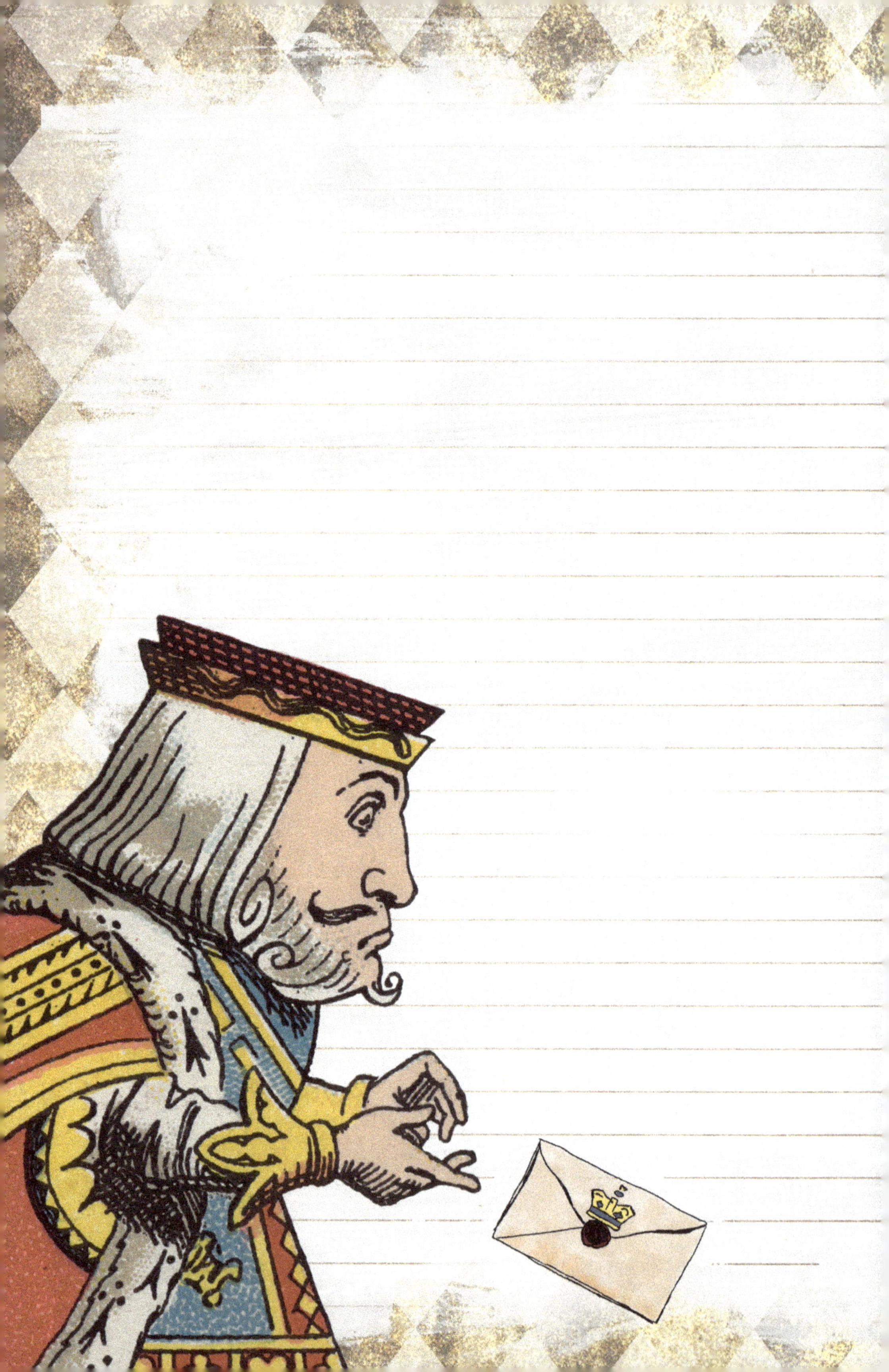

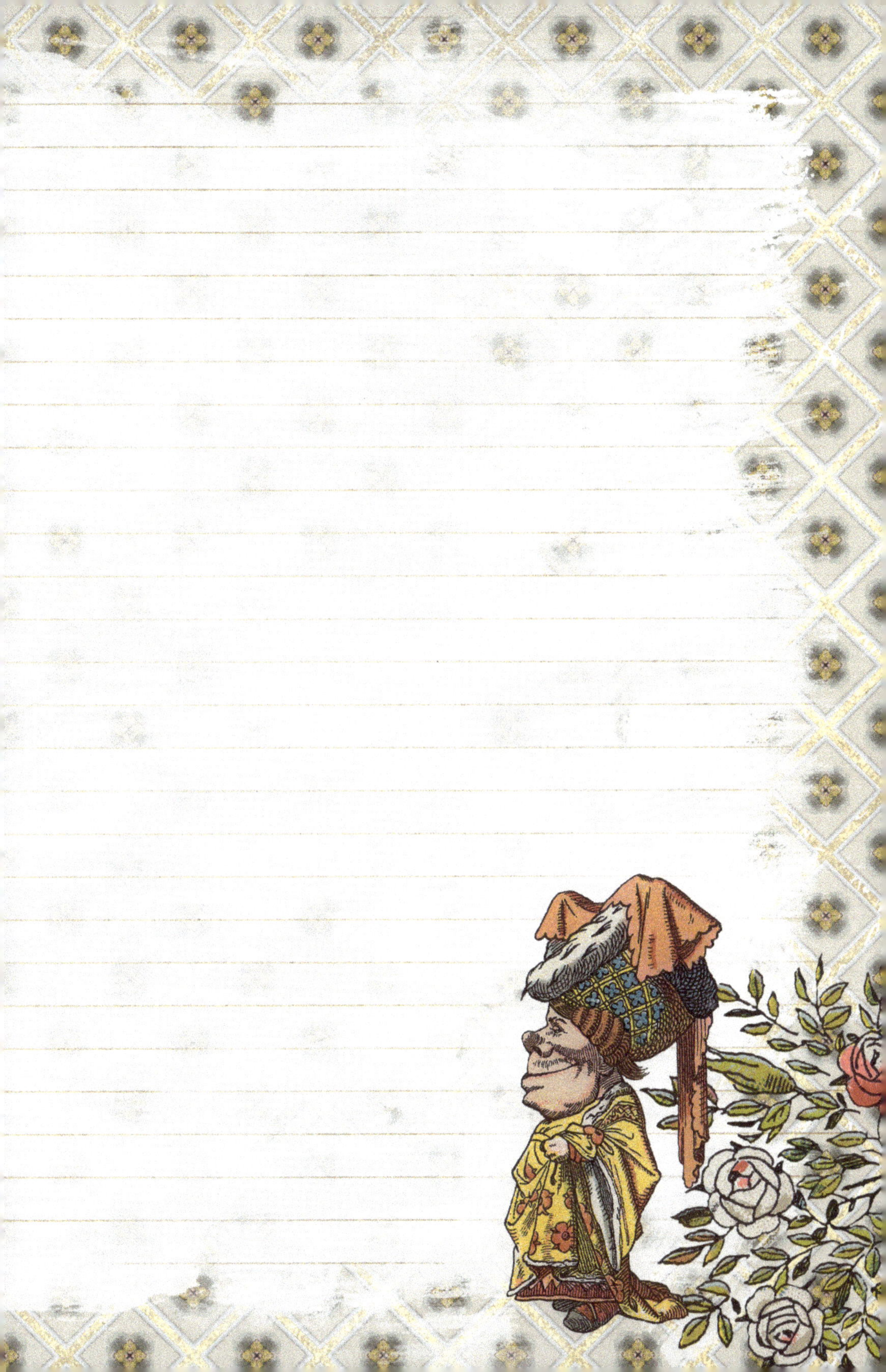

Curiouser
and
Curiouser

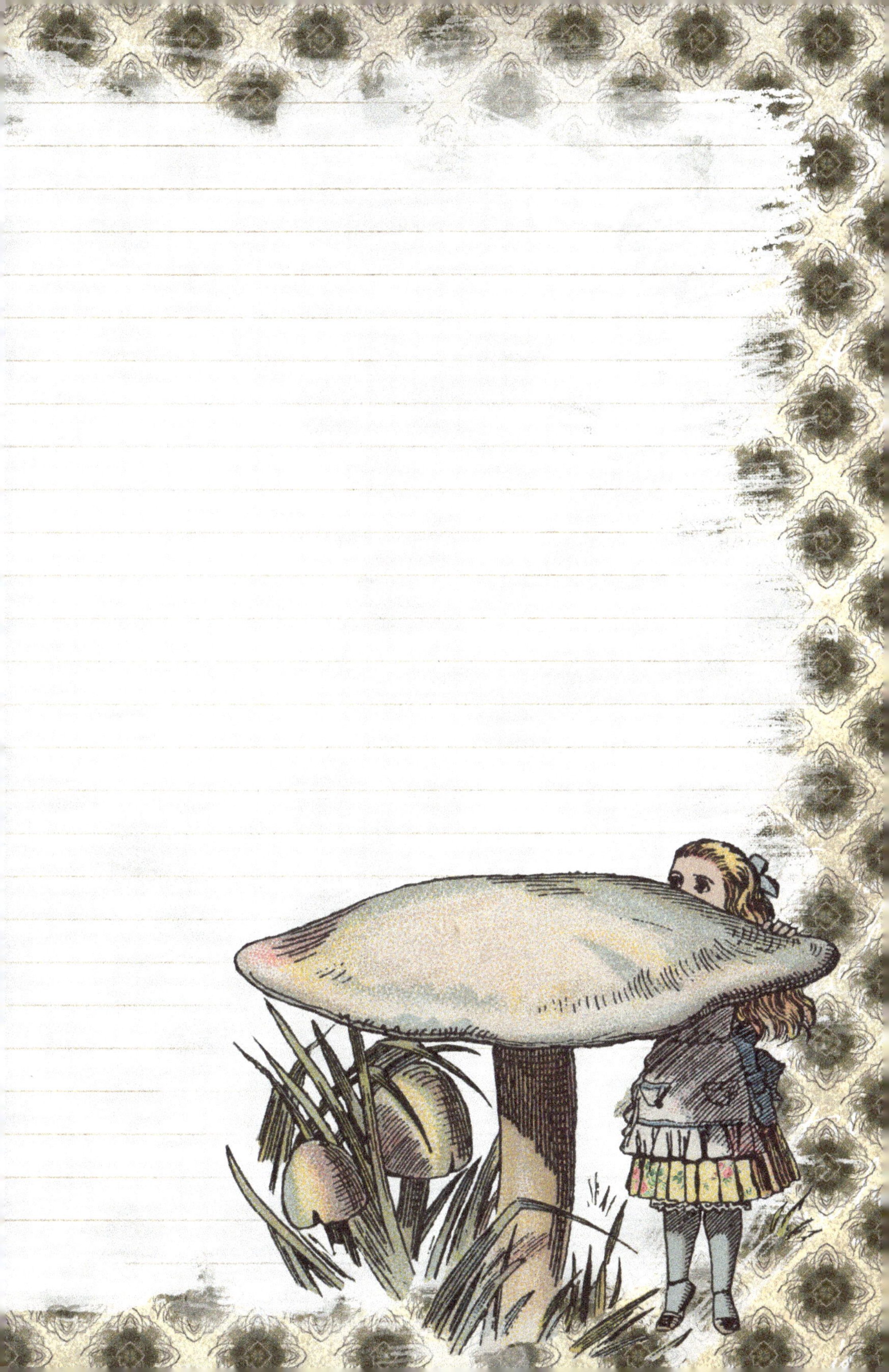

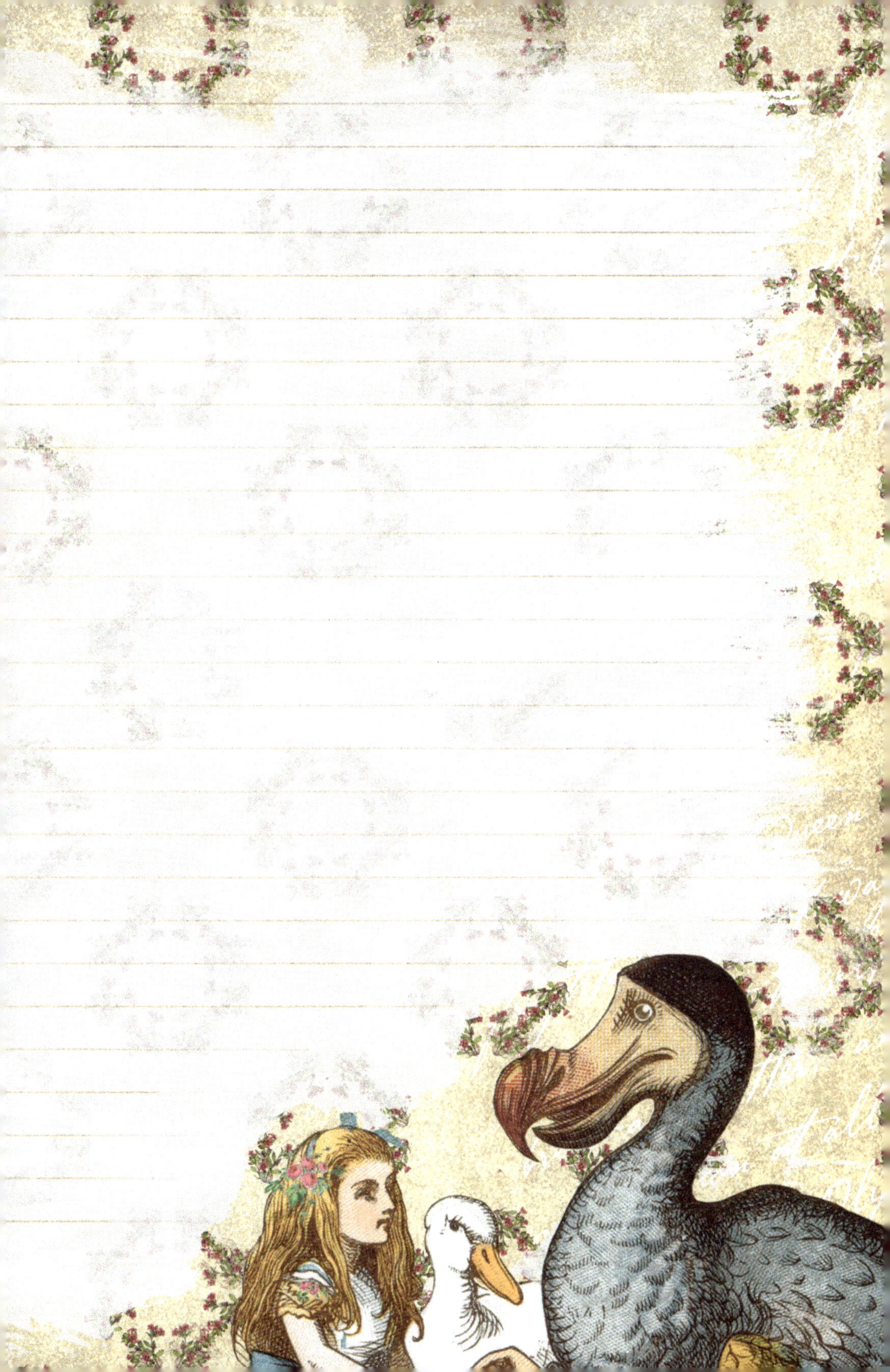

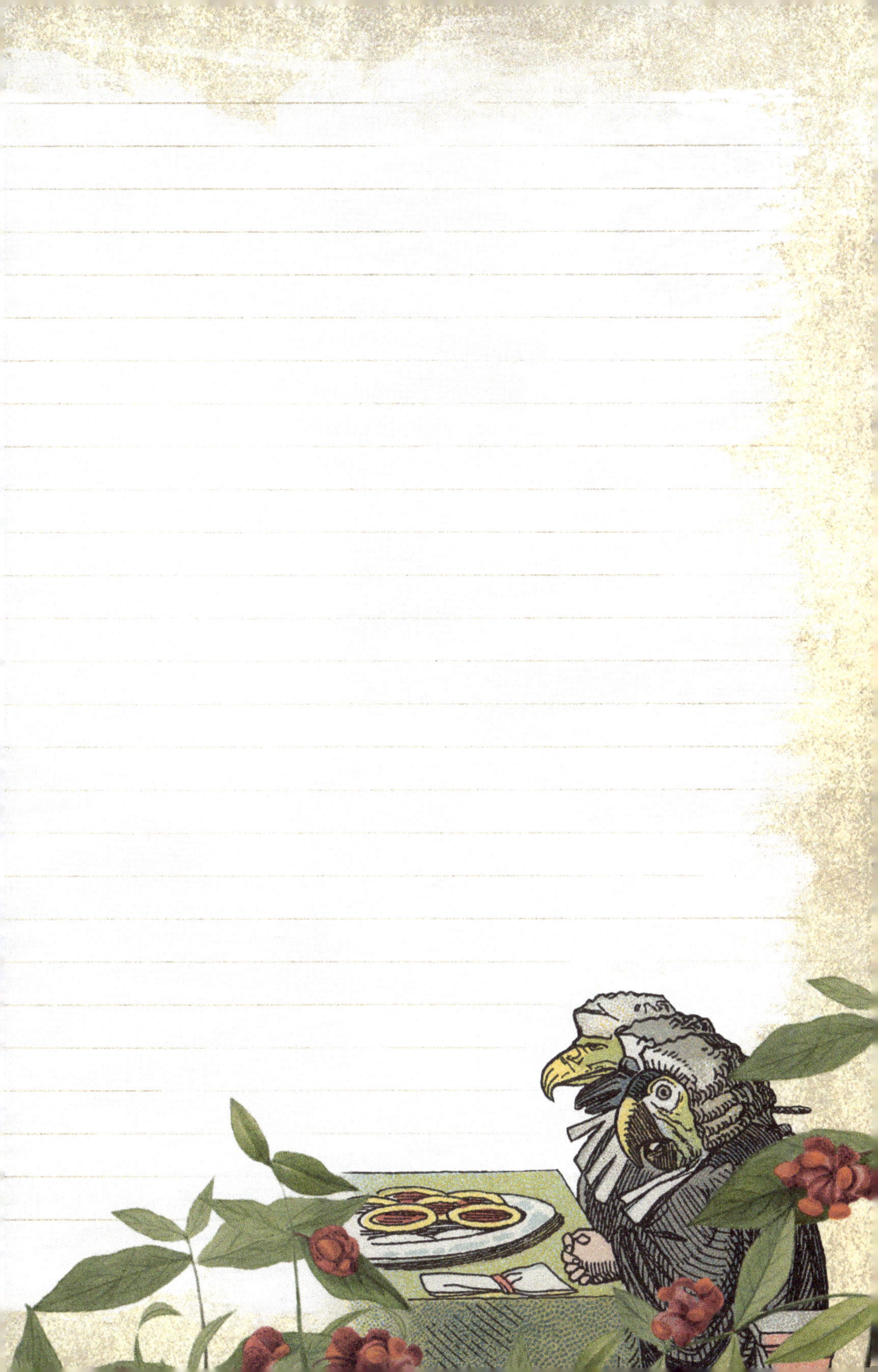

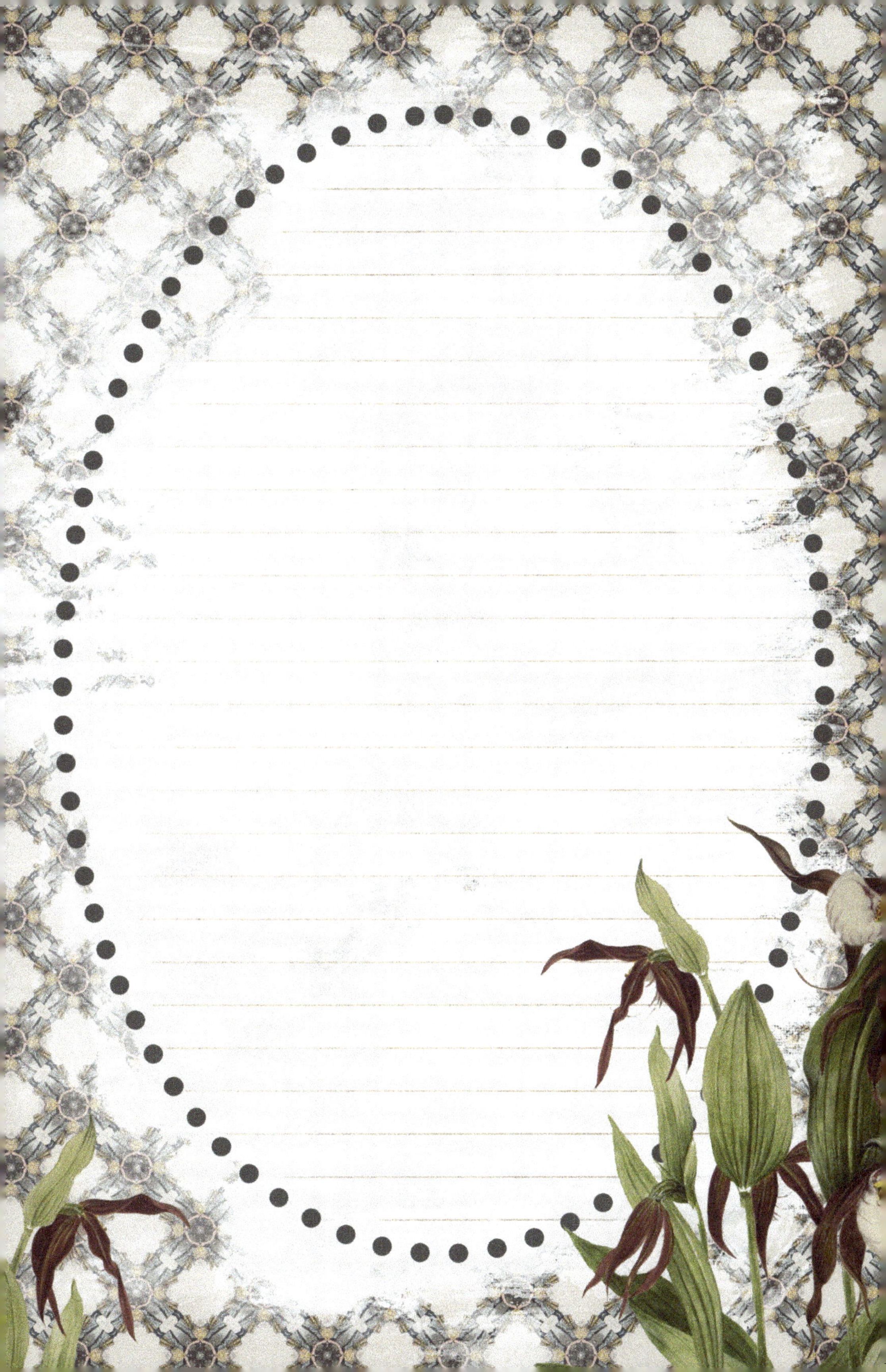

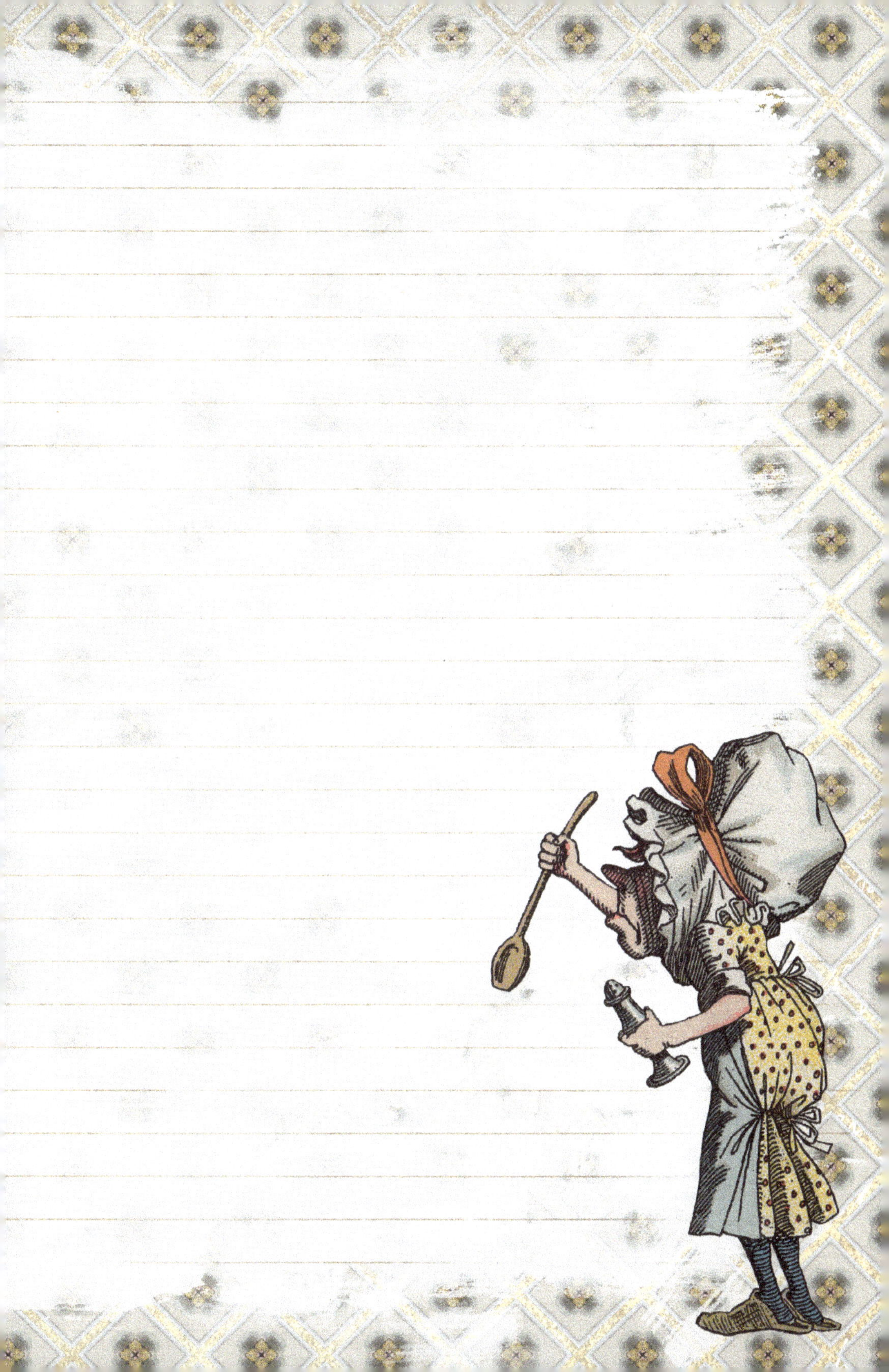

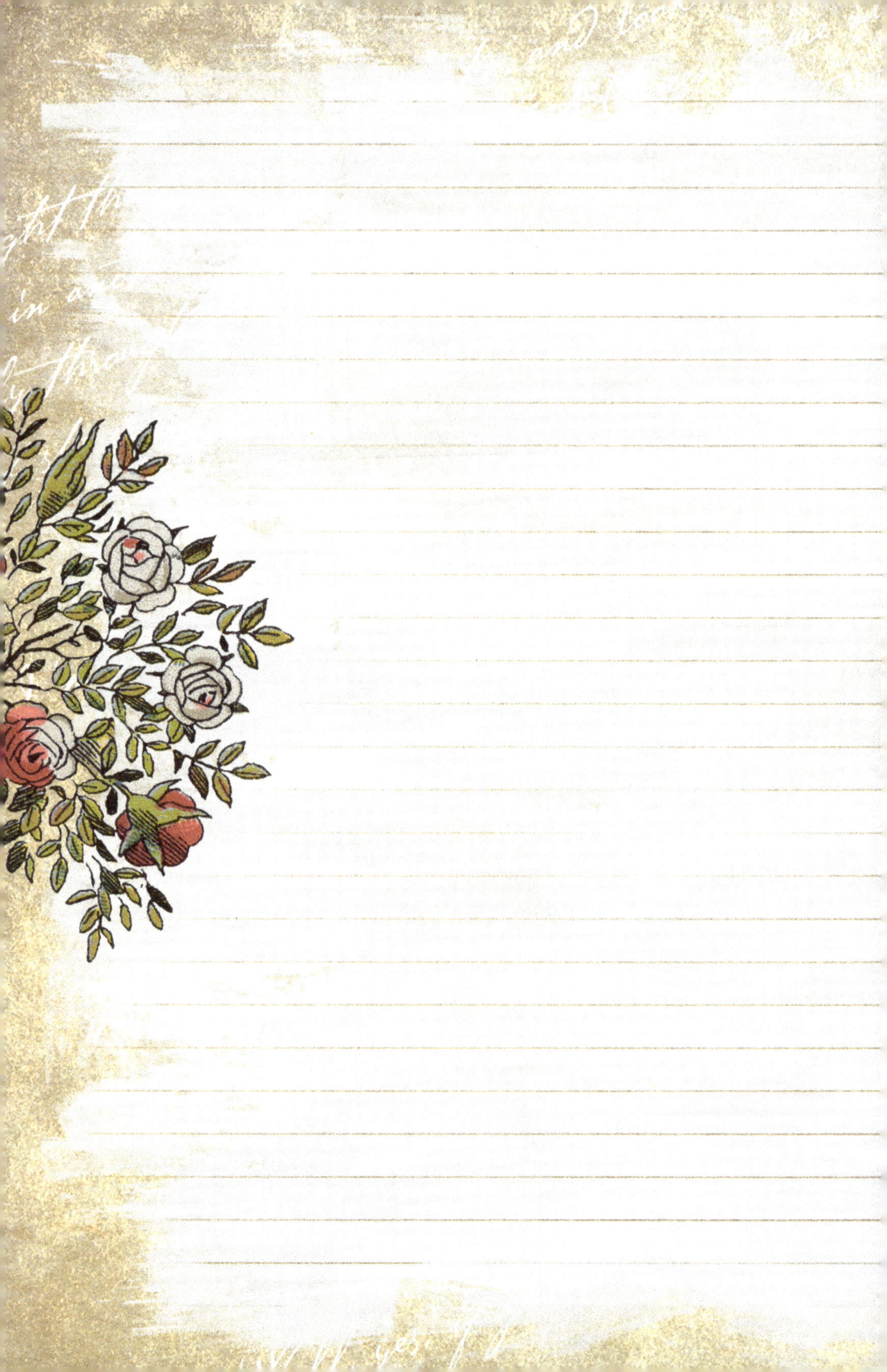

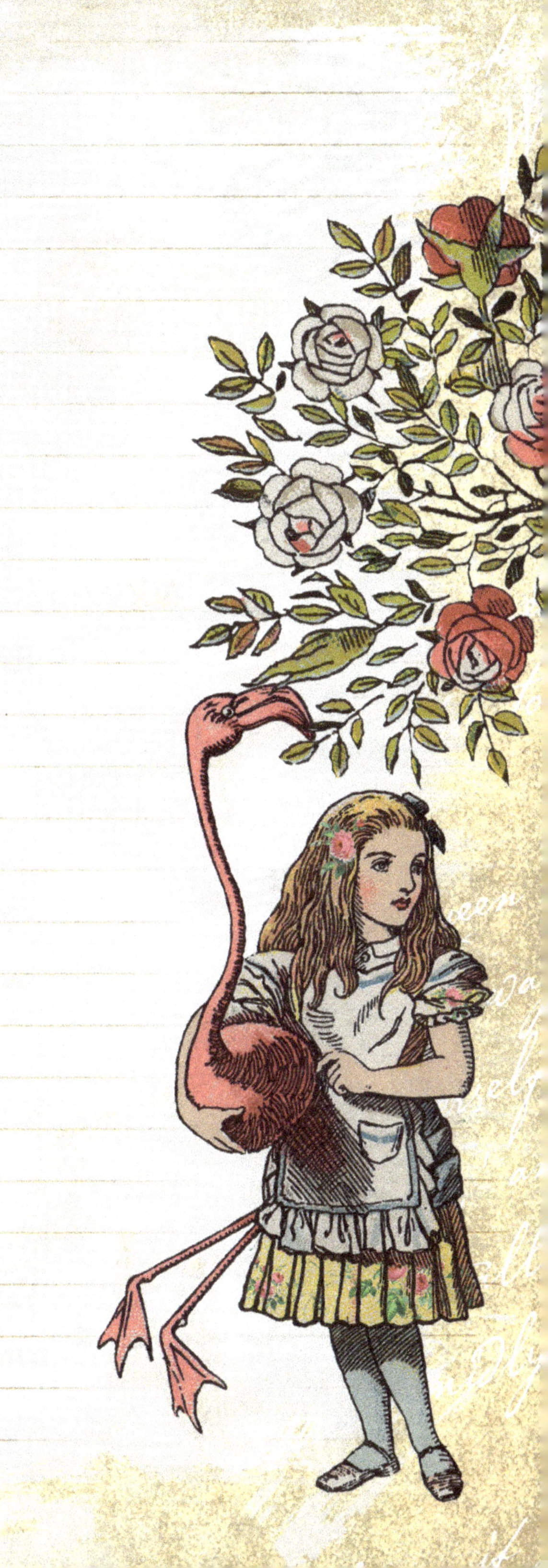

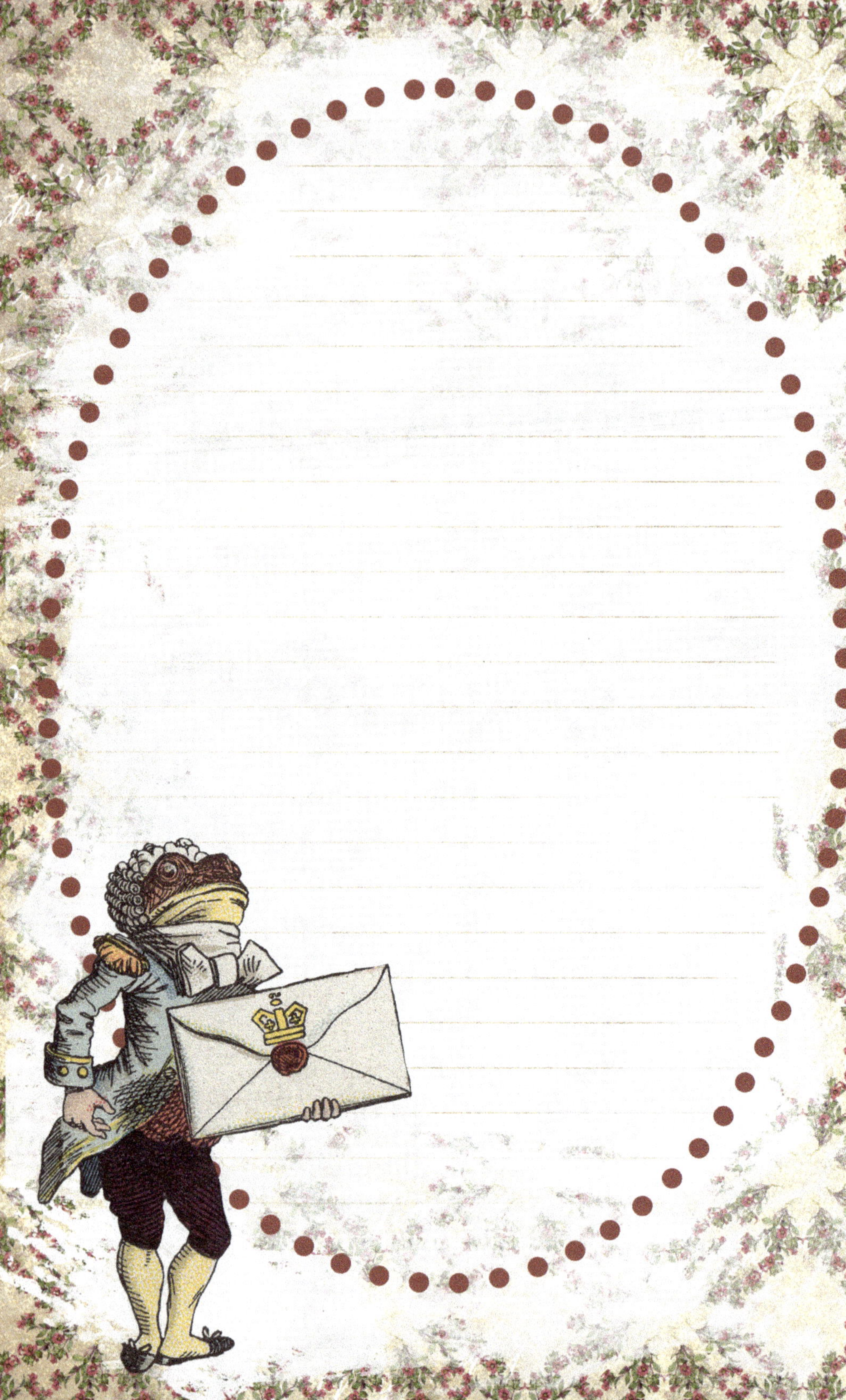

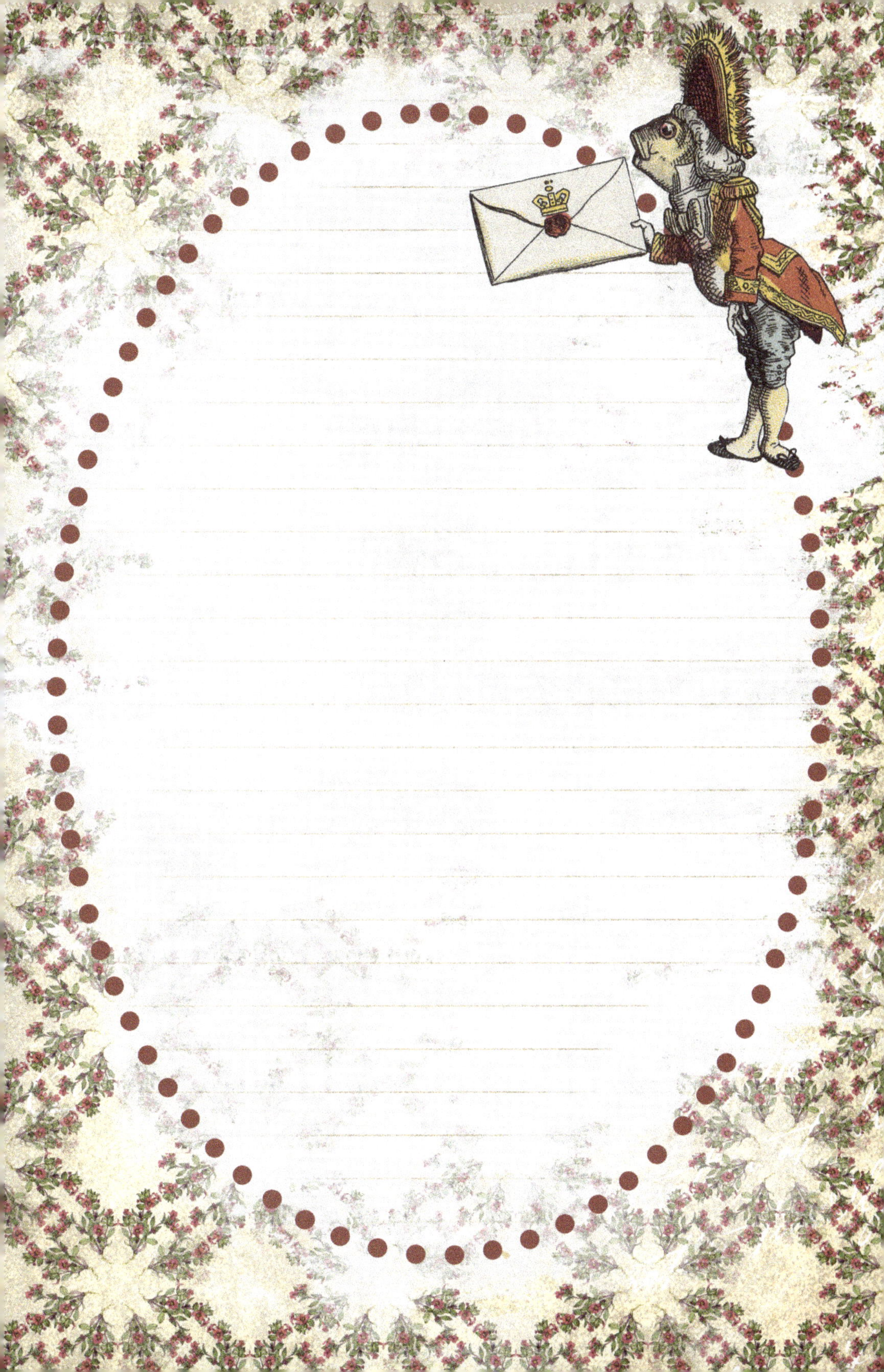

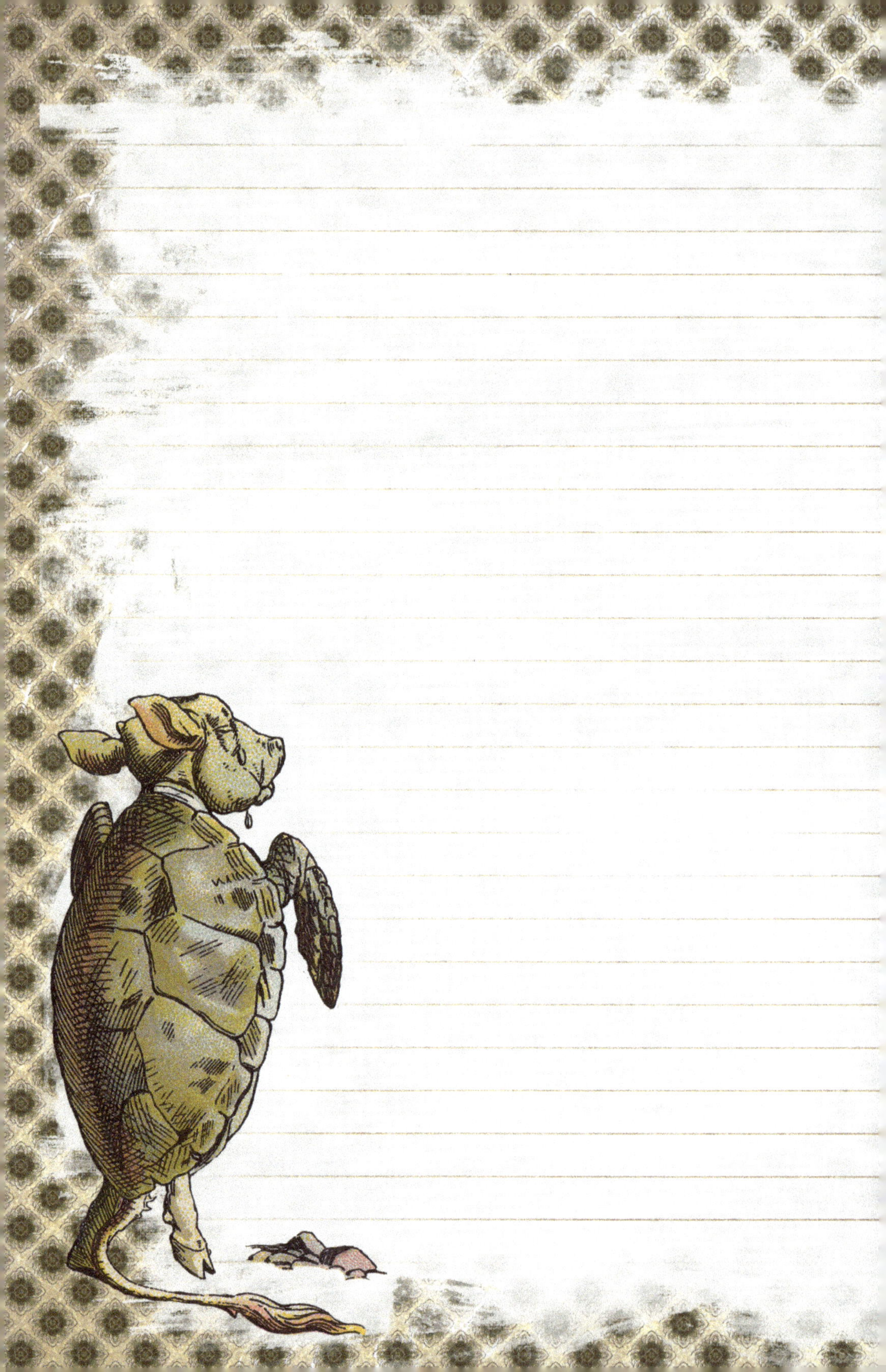

"Well!"
thought Alice
to herself,
"after such a fall
as this, I shall
think nothing of
tumbling down
stairs!"

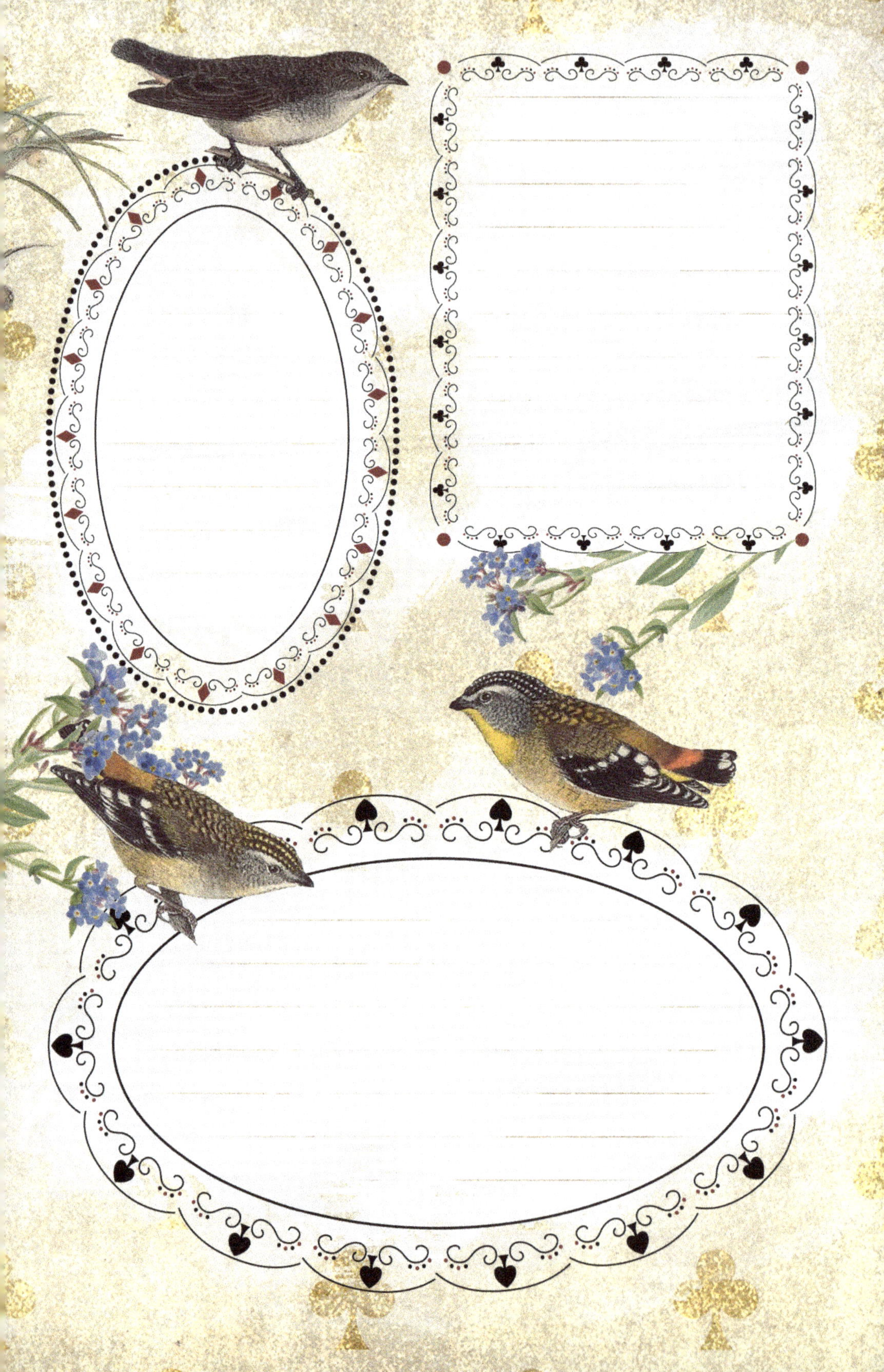

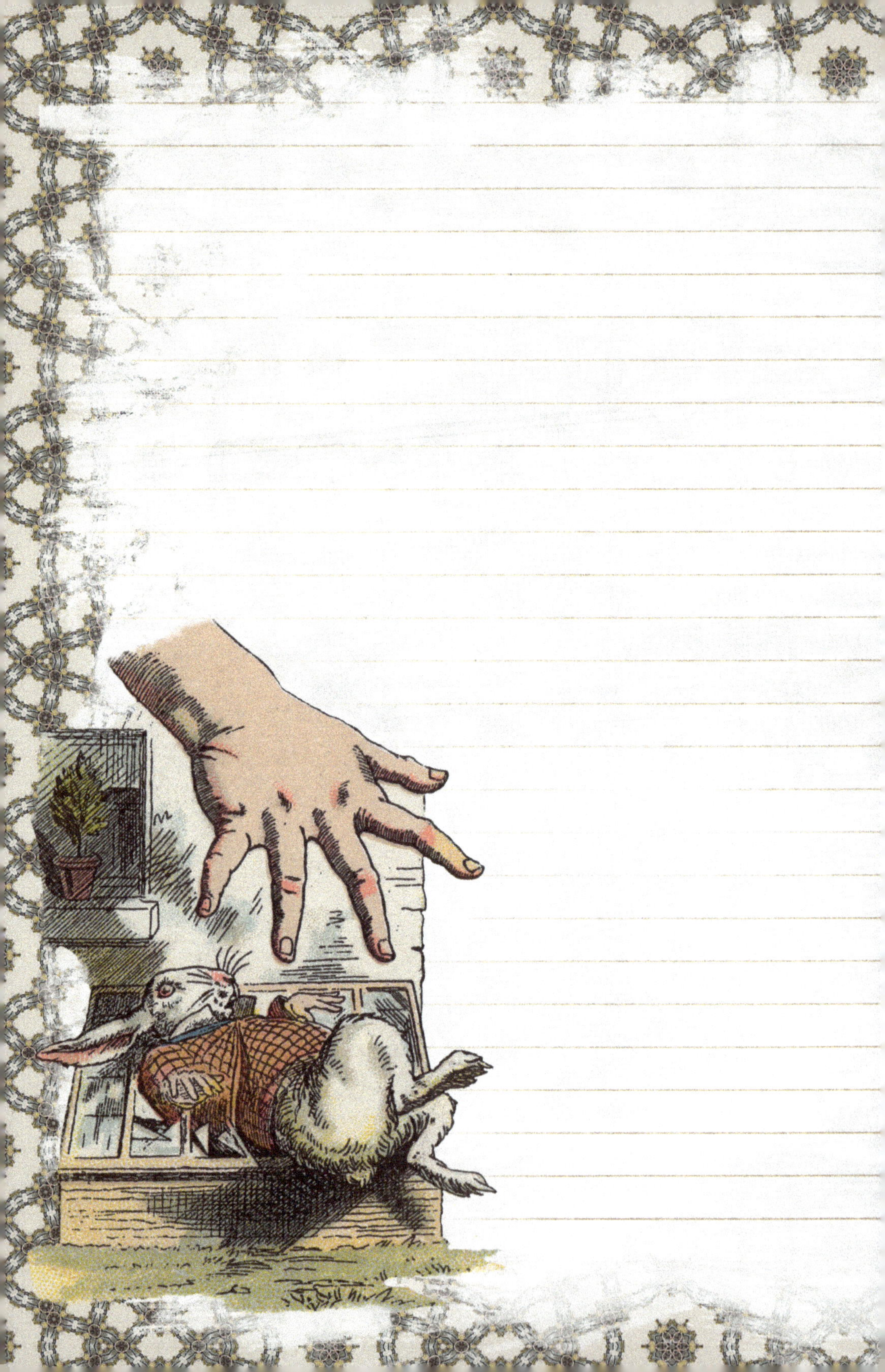

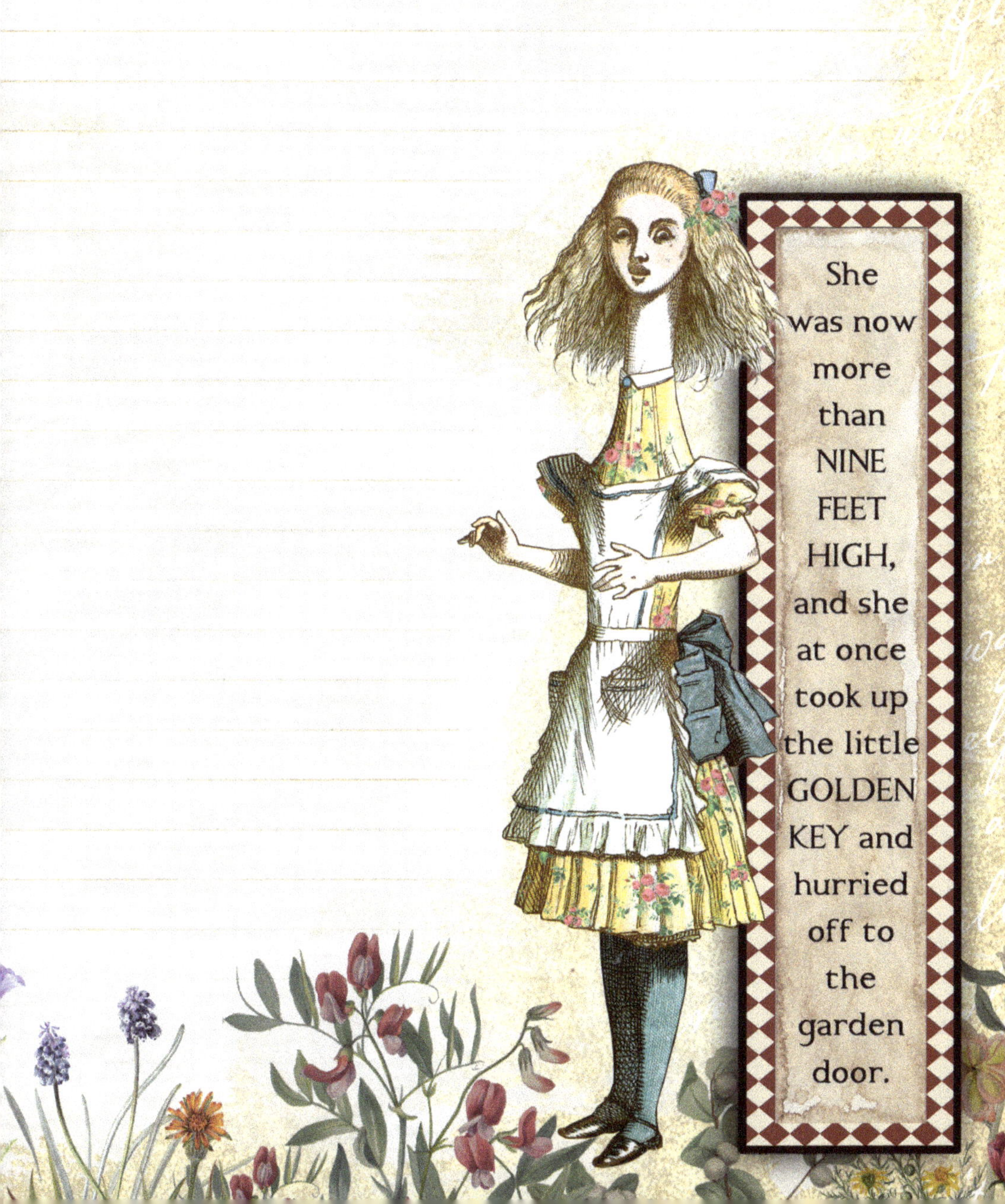

She was now more than NINE FEET HIGH, and she at once took up the little GOLDEN KEY and hurried off to the garden door.

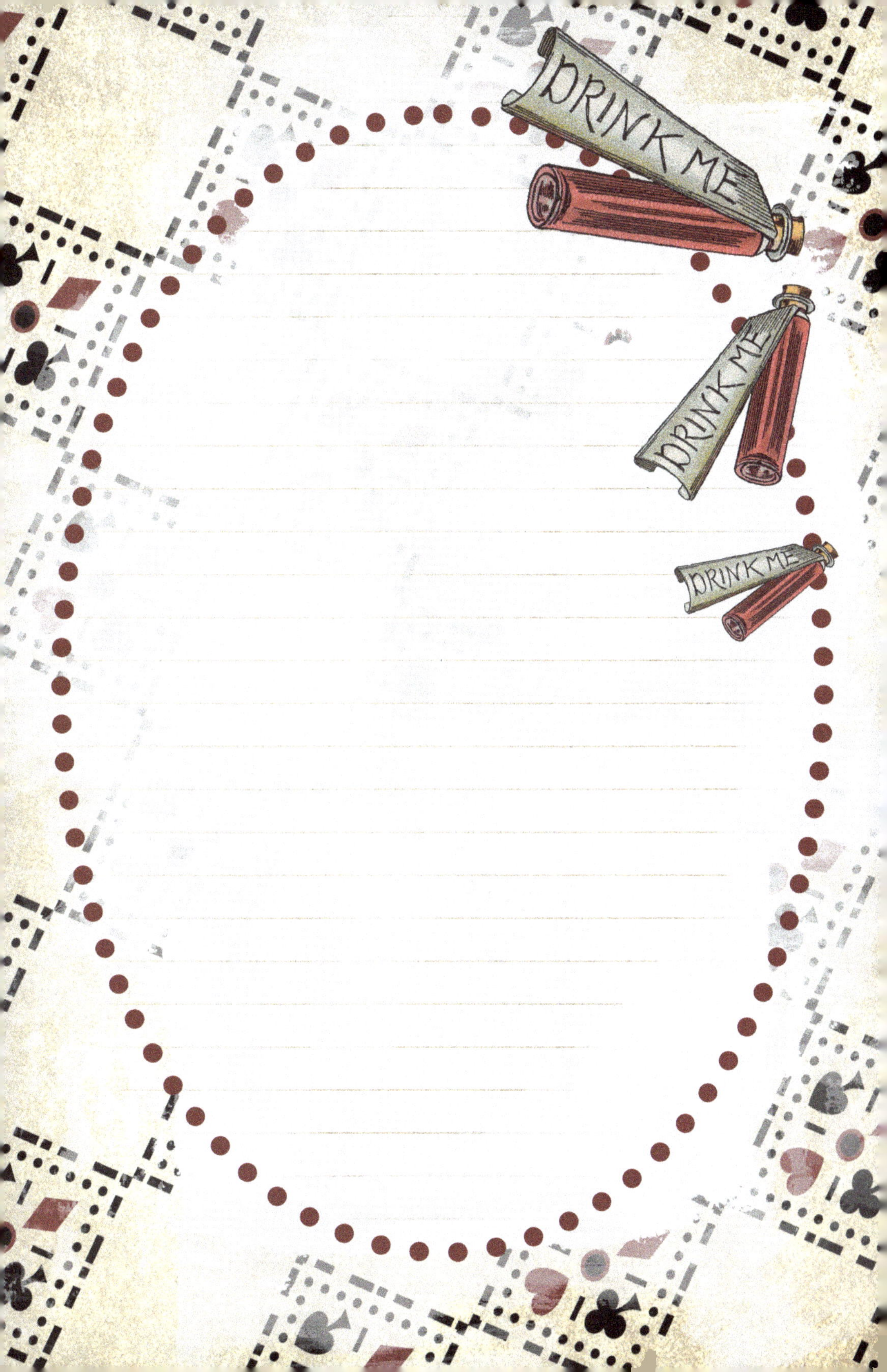
DRINK ME
DRINK ME
DRINK ME

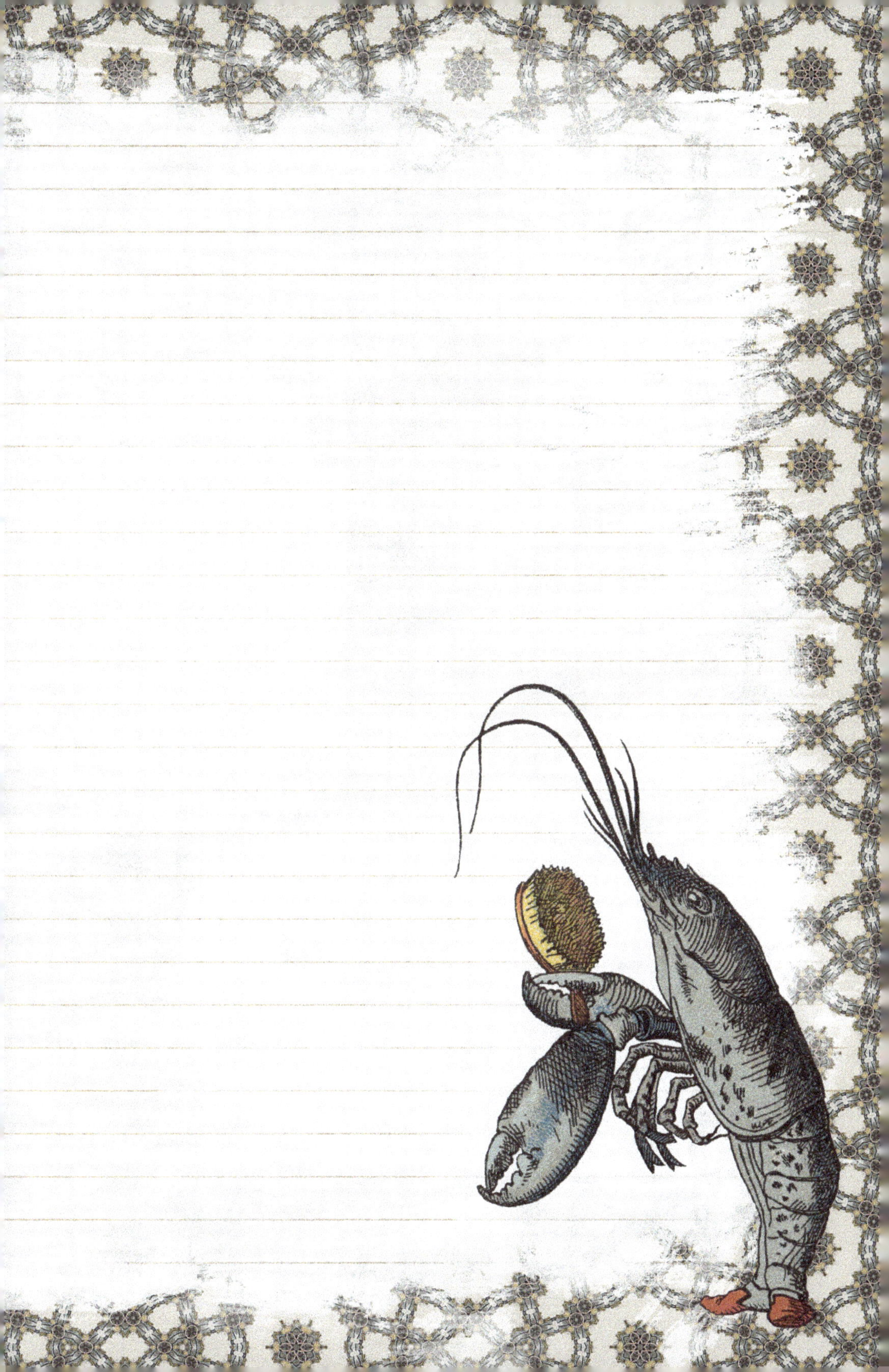

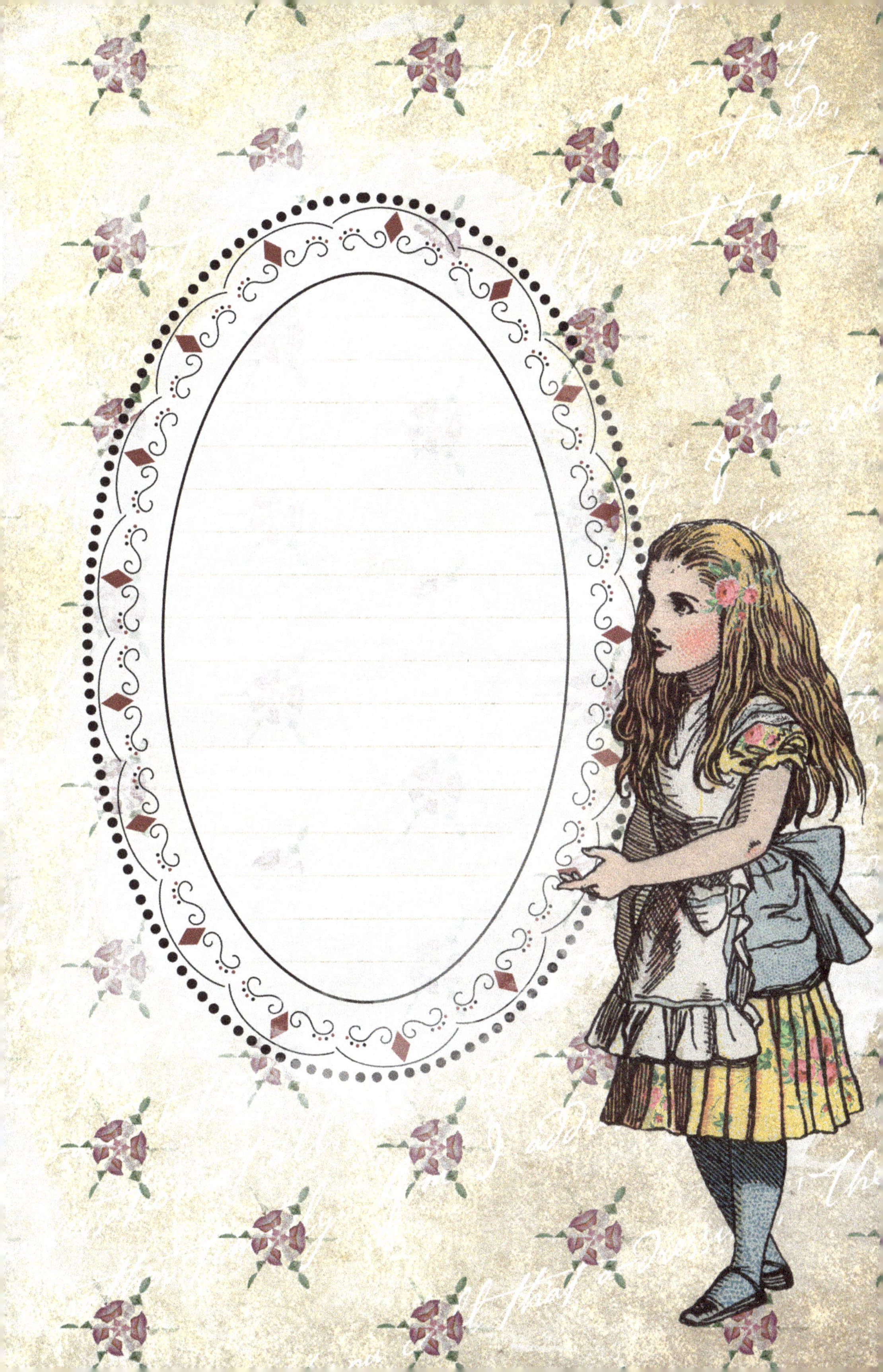

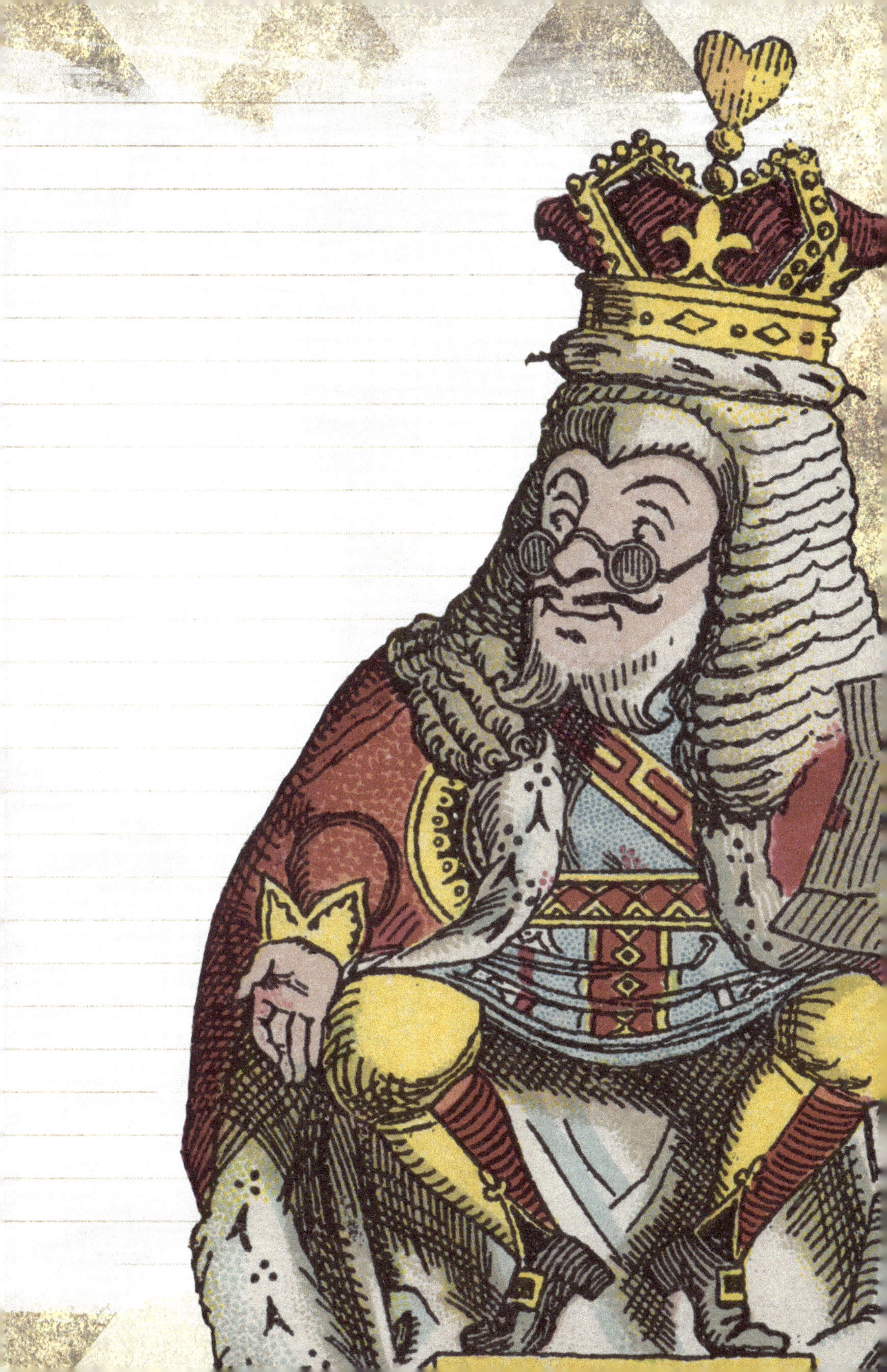

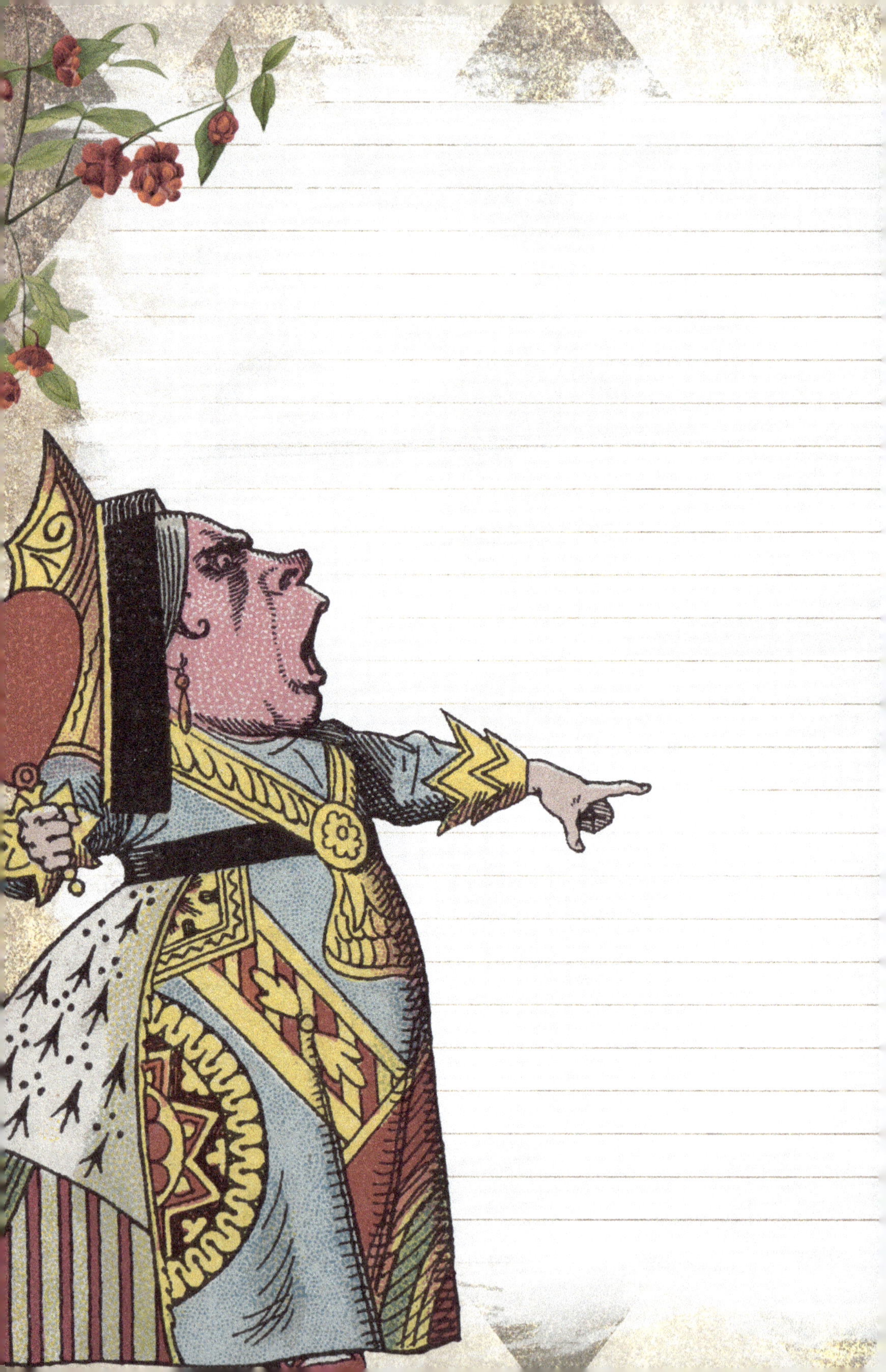

But the rabbit
was no longer to
be seen: she found
herself in a long,
low hall, which was
lit up by a row of
lamps hanging
from the roof

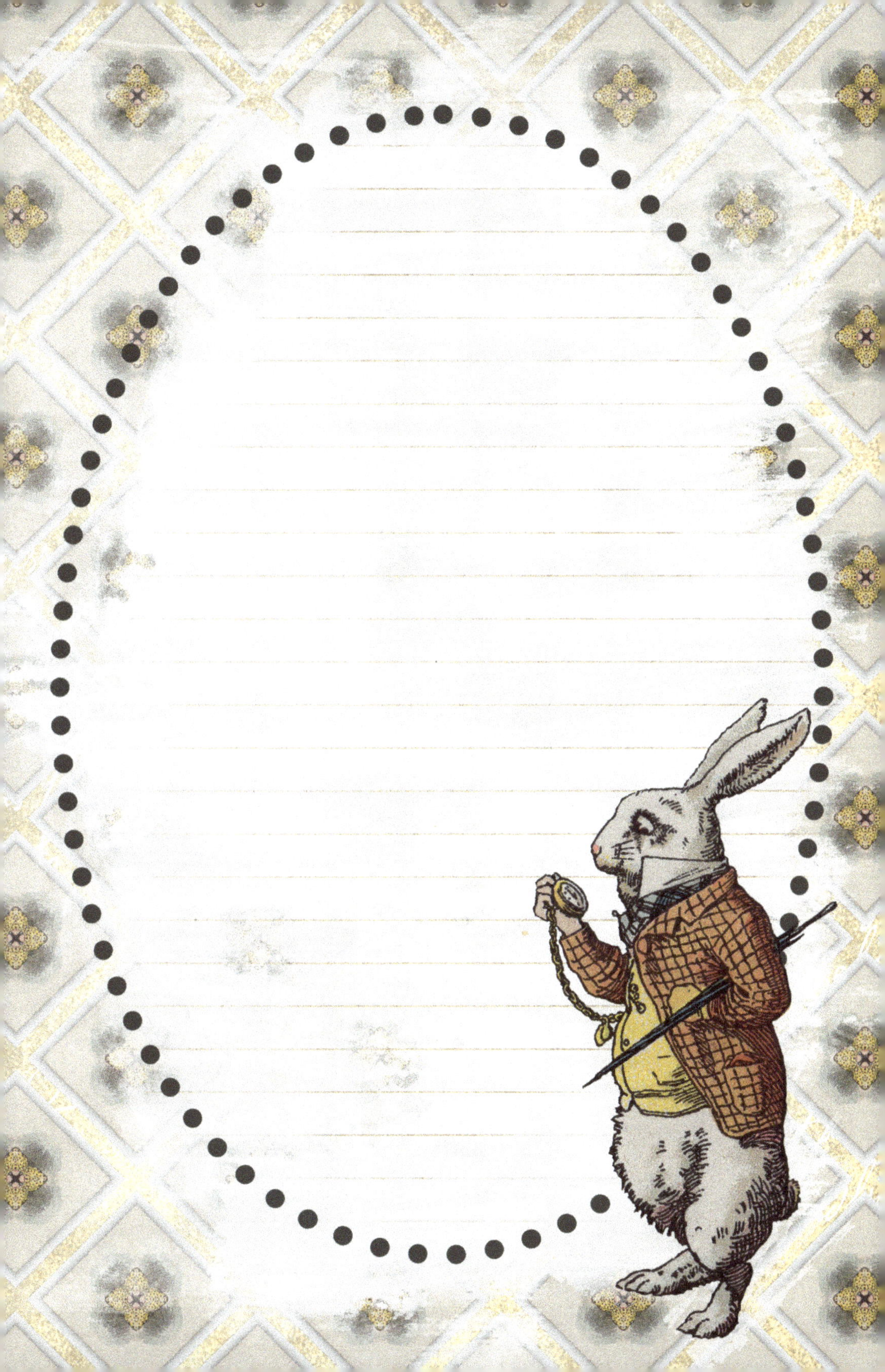

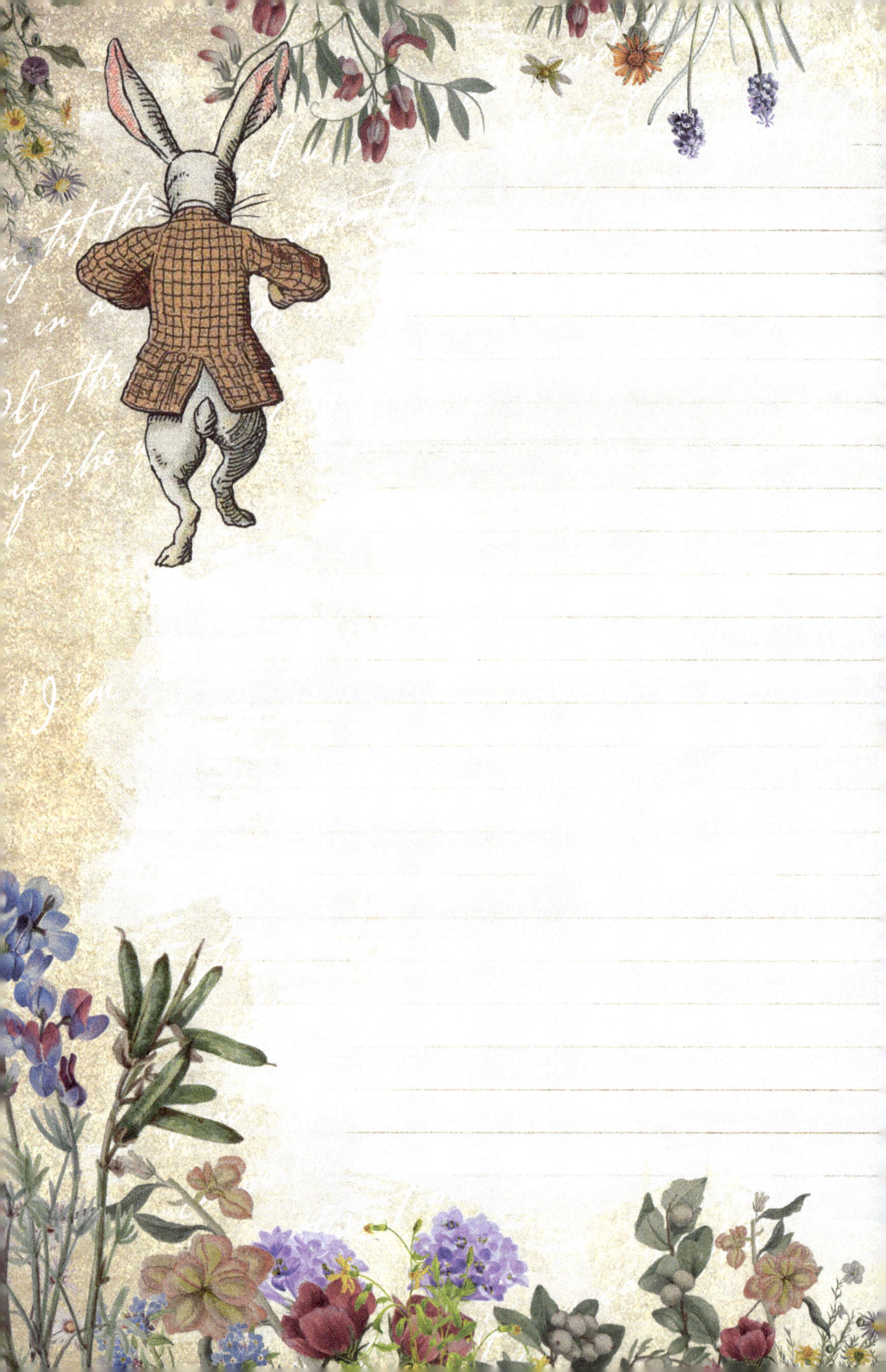

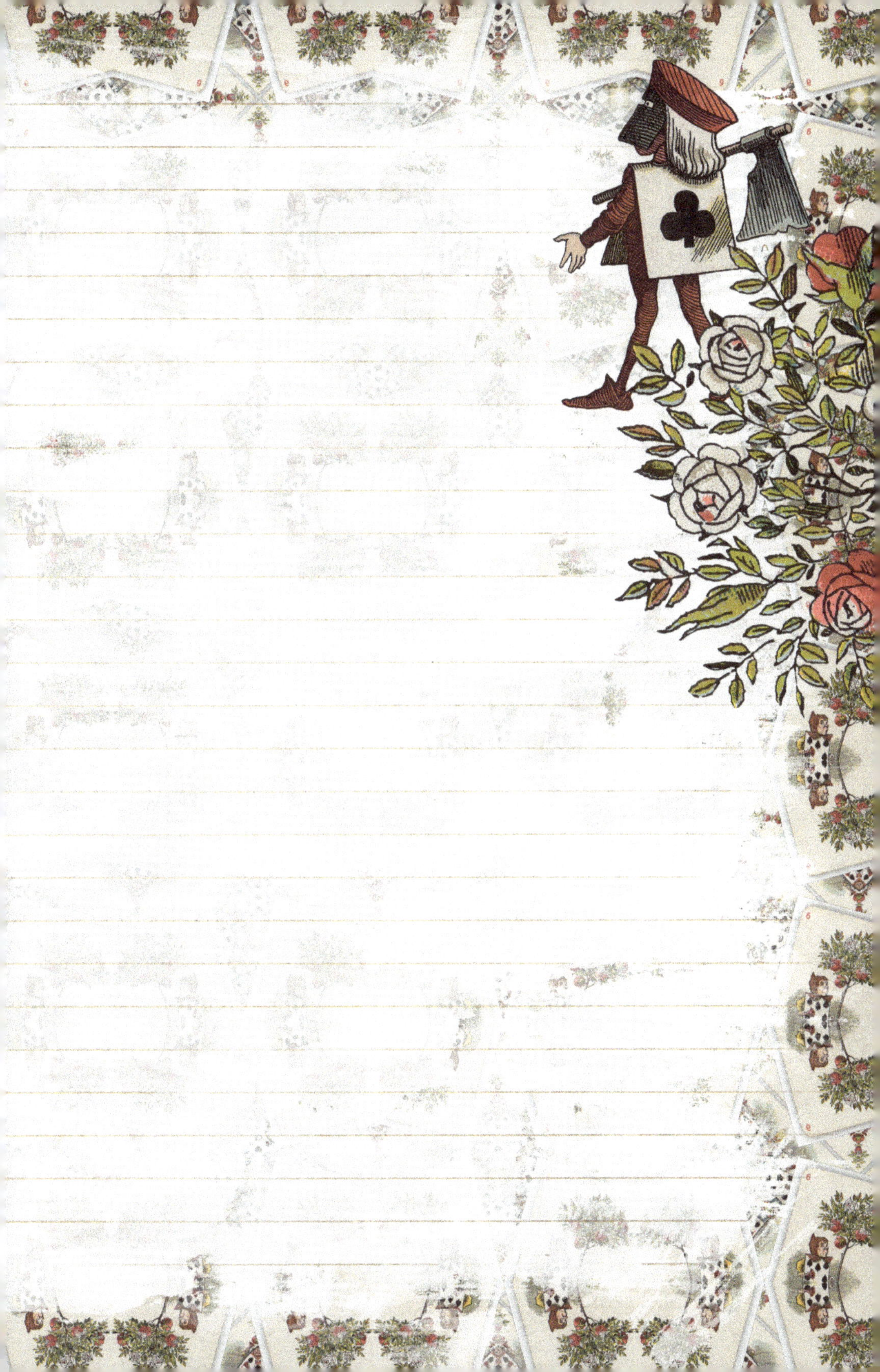

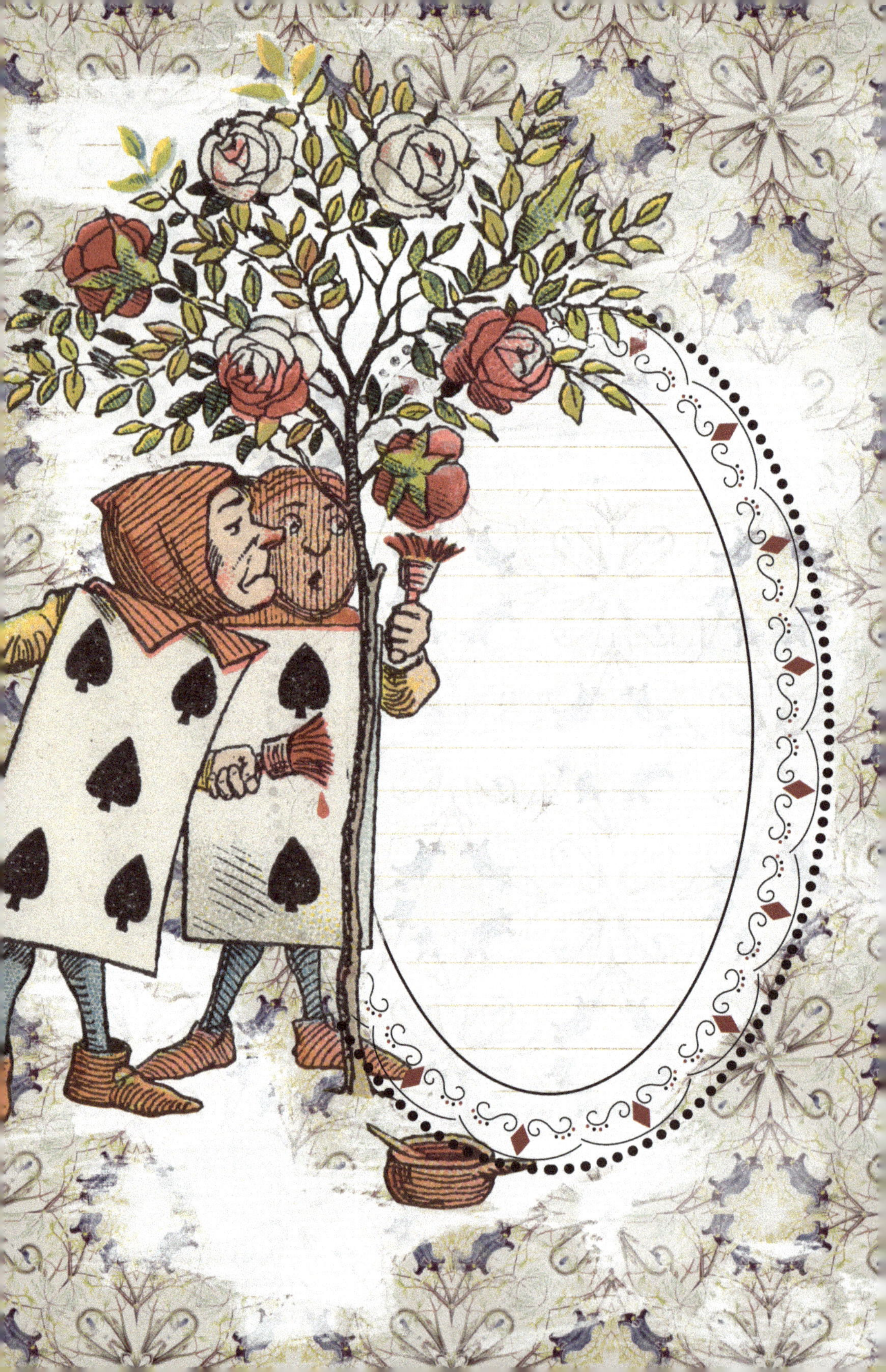

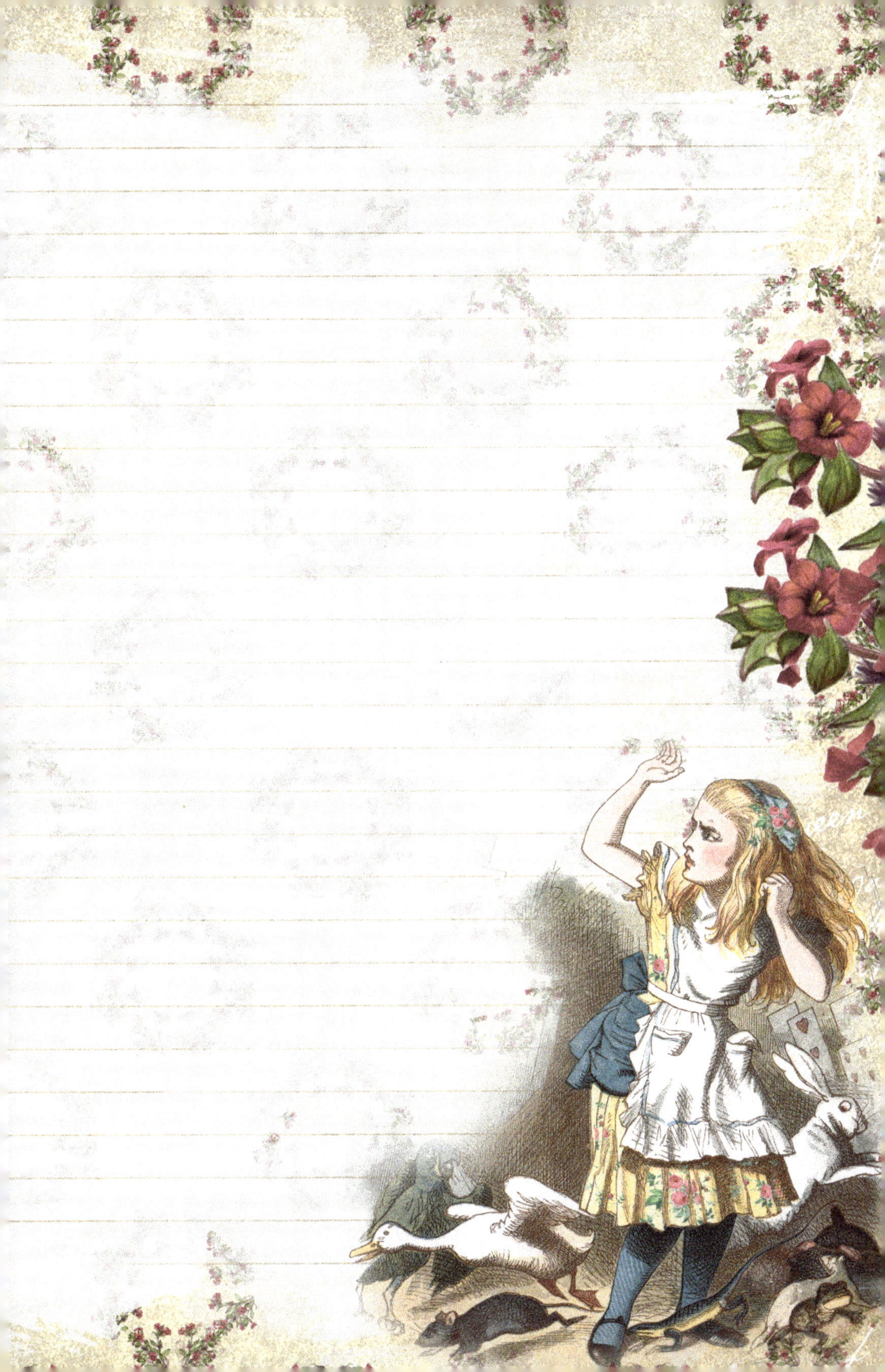

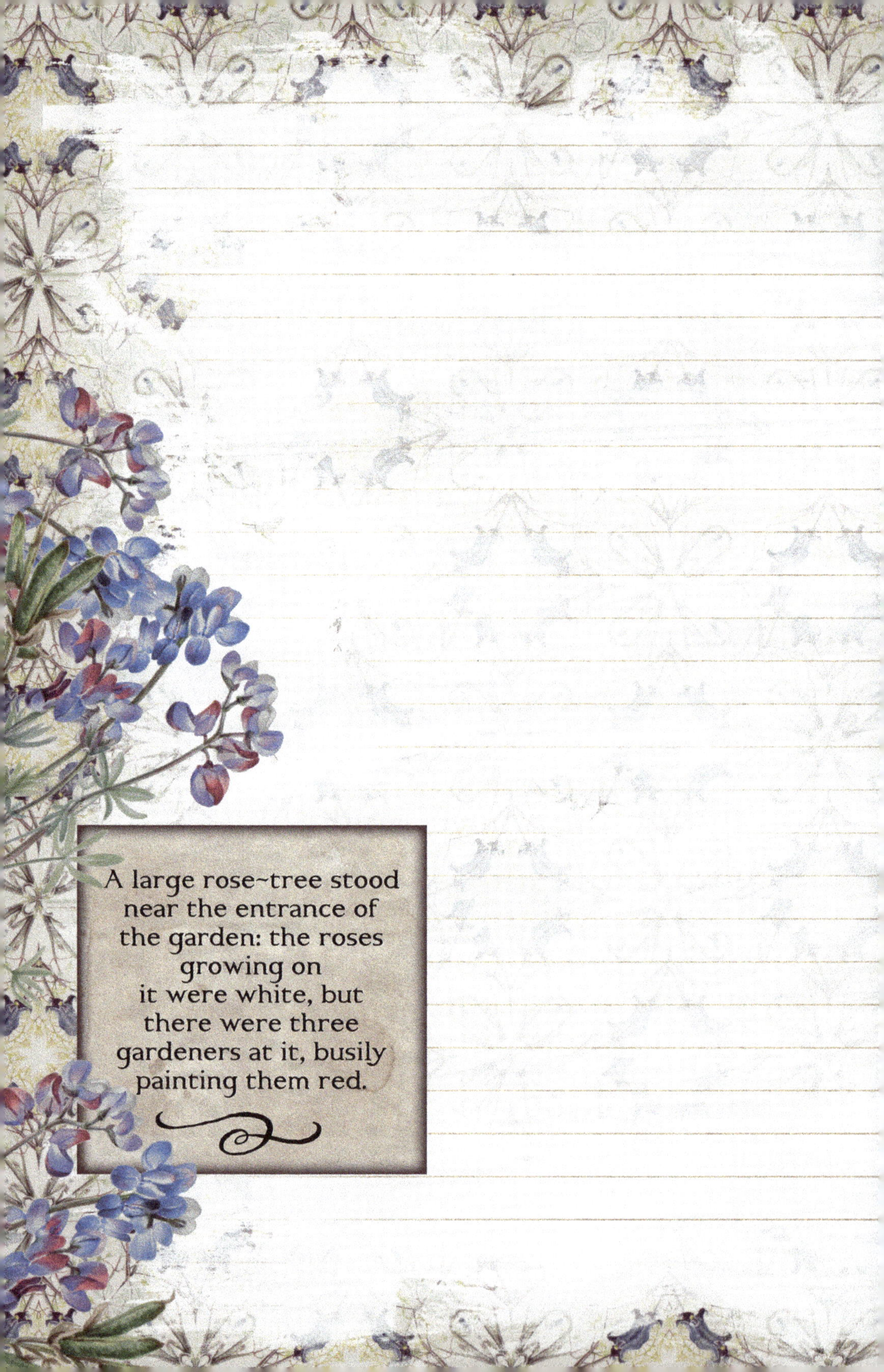

A large rose~tree stood
near the entrance of
the garden: the roses
growing on
it were white, but
there were three
gardeners at it, busily
painting them red.

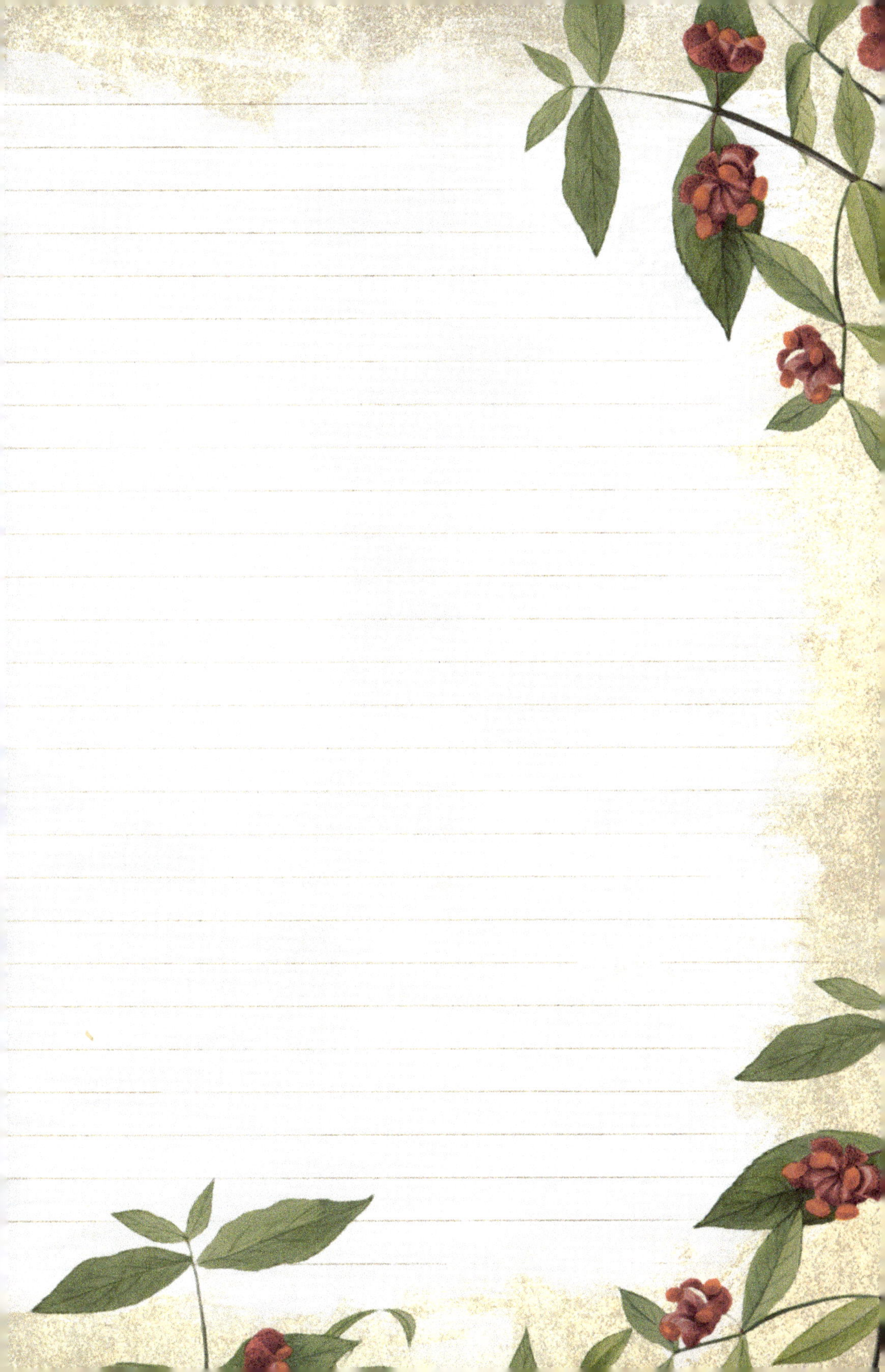

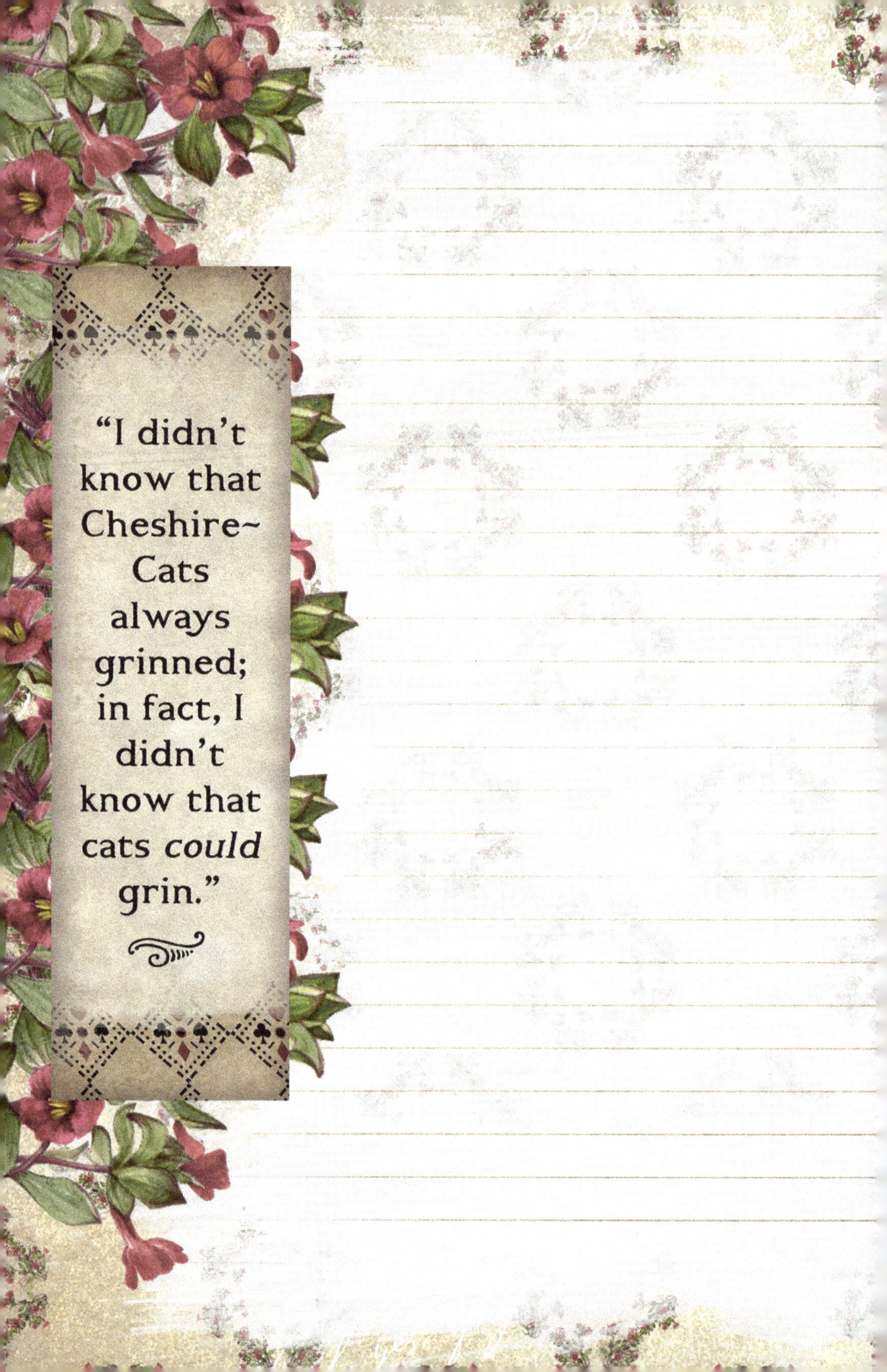

"I didn't know that Cheshire~ Cats always grinned; in fact, I didn't know that cats *could* grin."

Pen Test Page

About the Authors

Katie MacAlister

A *New York Times*, *USA Today*, and *Publishers Weekly* bestselling author, Katie MacAlister has always loved reading. Growing up in a family where a weekly visit to the library was a given, Katie spent much of her time with her nose buried in a book. Two years after she started writing novels, Katie sold her first romantic comedy. More than sixty books later, her novels have been translated into numerous languages, been recorded as audiobooks, received several awards, and are regulars on the bestseller lists. Katie was a member of the Lewis Carroll Society of North America for many years, and now lives in the Pacific Northwest with two dogs, and can often be found lurking around online.

L.K. Glover

A graphic design artist and owner of Ninth Moon, LLC, L.K. has a passion for innovative products, whimsical details, and is known for running with scissors and refusing to stay within the lines. She lives in the Pacific Northwest with her husband and son. A herd of wild rabbits have been known to frolic in her back yard.

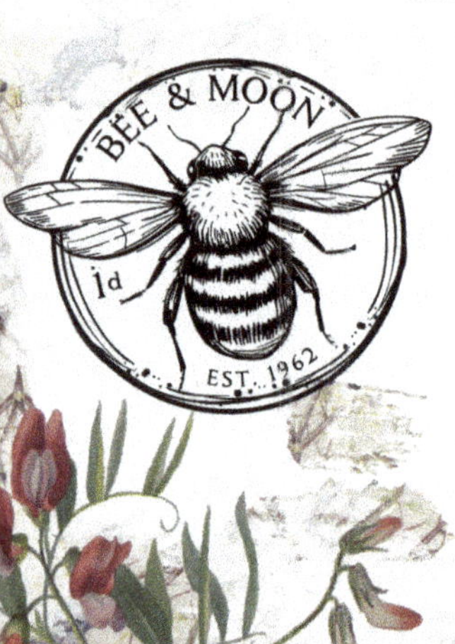

Bee & Moon

L.K. and Katie were brought together by a love of writing, and have remained friends for almost twenty years. They share a passion for crafting, deep and abiding love of chocolate, and an appreciation for all things Alice. In 2020 they formed Bee & Moon as their brand for their Alice and related projects.